Discover Maths

AF621112

PRACTISE & PASS 11+ LEVEL ONE: DISCOVER MATHS

	Frequently asked questions for adults	2
LESSON 1	Finding the place value with whole numbers and decimals	5
LESSON 2	Calculating fractions of a whole number	13
LESSON 3	Finding the whole number from a fraction	21
LESSON 4	Simplifying fractions	29
LESSON 5	Adding and subtracting with decimals	37
LESSON 6	Turning fractions into decimals and percentages	45
LESSON 7	Calculating probability	53
LESSON 8	Calculating ratios	61
LESSON 9	Calculating proportion	69
LESSON 10	Calculating areas and perimeters	77
LESSON 11	Calculating the area of right-angled triangles and irregular shapes	85
LESSON 12	Calculating angles	93
LESSON 13	Multiplying money and decimals	101
LESSON 14	Finding averages and ranges	108
LESSON 15	Finding a percentage of a number	117
	Score sheet	124
	Metric measures	124
	Vocabulary builder	125
	And finally...	126
	Answers to part 2 questions	127

Frequently Asked Questions For Adults

What is this book about?

Discover Maths is in level one of the *Practise & Pass 11+* series. It is a workbook for students who are going to take an 11+ test or school entrance exam that includes a maths section. In the book I introduce them to 15 key types of question they'll typically face in the exam and provide 300 questions for practice.

I provide coaching for students throughout the book. I talk them through the whole process, from answering questions to helping them understand their mistakes, so that they have a firm understanding of the basics.

How do I use this book?

This book is divided into bite-sized lessons for the students to work through. Each lesson covers a specific type of question and is set up in the same way:

1. I explain the question type, giving the student an understanding of what they need to know.
2. I provide 1 or 2 worked examples to show how the question type is best tackled.

   (Note: I recommend that an adult reads through the explanation and example(s) with the student to ensure they have a firm understanding of what is required. It is possible that the method I suggest is different to the one the student may have used at school. In this case talk to the student to make sure they use the method they are happiest with.)
3. When ready, the student should work through the first set of practice questions on their own and mark their answers on the answer sheet provided.
4. The answers to the questions are included on the following page. Once the student has completed the practice questions they can mark their answers themselves.
5. After the answers I provide a summary of what the student's score means and give hints on how to improve it, if needs be.

   (Note: the student should discuss any errors and talk through the hints with an adult so that any problems are dealt with straight away.)
6. Next, there is a second set of practice questions which makes up part 2 of the lesson. The student should only work on these when they understand why they made mistakes in part 1.

   Important: the second set of questions should be marked by an adult and the answers can be found on pages 127 and 128. You might want to cut these out of the book so the temptation for the student to take a peek is removed!
7. Finally there is a score sheet on page 124 which should be completed after each lesson to keep a record of progress. This can be used to identify the question types the student needs to practise more.

   (Note: occasionally I will include a question that hasn't been explained in the lesson. This is by design: the student will very likely come up against a question they are not familiar with in the actual test so it's important that they get used to applying the knowledge they have to work out the right answer.)

Why does this book feature multiple choice answers?

Multiple choice answers are becoming the most common format for the 11+ and entrance exams. This means that 5 possible answers are given for each question and they are presented to the student in a grid. To answer the question correctly the student has to put a horizontal line in the empty box next to the correct answer.

- It's important that students learn to use these grids correctly from the outset so that they avoid making common errors, such as marking the wrong box or accidentally missing out questions.
- Do make sure you find out from the examination centre whether the multiple choice format is to be used in the final exam so you are confident that the student is doing the right preparation.

When should the student start to prepare for the exam and how often should they practise?

The sooner the student starts to prepare for the exam the better. Realistically I suggest there should be a full year's run-up to the test so that the student has a chance to practise all of the subject areas and question types that might appear in the exam without having to study for hours and hours each week. This means working through all three levels of the *Practise & Pass 11+* series (this book is in level one of the series) at a steady and realistic pace.

For this book I recommend students work at the pace of 1 lesson a week which means 15 weeks in total. However, if a student is able, there is nothing to stop them moving through the book at a quicker pace.

What's the best way for a student to study?

- It's important that the student gets used to a test-type environment so make sure there's a clear space to work in, with no distractions. This means the TV and all music should be switched off, the student should be sat at a table and there should be a clock in clear view so that they can time themselves.
- Students should use a pencil to answer the questions and have an eraser and some scrap paper to hand which they can use for any workings out.

  (Note: I highly recommend that the student avoid practising on the same days that they have school homework and that they also have other extra-curricular activities – this means they have other outlets for their energies and don't become overworked, stressed or too bored with the practice.)

How quickly should a student answer the questions?

I have suggested timings for each lesson but do note that, as this book is in level one of the series, the timings here are more generous than they will be in the actual exam. At this stage students should concentrate on becoming familiar with the question types and their methods – they can ignore the timings for the time-being if they wish.

Once students are used to the questions they can then practise speeding up. At level two of the series I expect the students to be up to speed and they should follow the timings far more closely (this way they are prepared to work at a 'real time' pace that matches the actual exam).

What score should the student be aiming for?

Remember that 11+ tests and entrance examinations are tough to pass. I have written this book to reflect that fact, so it is unlikely that the student will sail through the book scoring 100% in each lesson.

After the first set of practice questions in every lesson, I have given a target score for that particular question type – this is based on my experience of teaching them year on year and should help you assess how the student is doing, and what, if any, areas need work. I also include helpful tips on how students can improve, and would recommend they use the 'vocabulary builder' on page 125 to note down any new words they come across.

I should add that the scores here in no way indicate whether the student will definitely pass or fail the exam; they are only here as a guide.

What is the 'vocabulary builder'?

There is a vocabulary builder exercise on page 125. This is an extra task to help improve the student's vocabulary.

What should I do once this book is completed?

This book is just the start; I recommend that you move on to level two of the series: *Develop Maths*. In level two there are many more practice questions covering more question types and trickier versions of questions that stretch the student further and improve their familiarity with what's expected from them on test day. There is also further advice from me on how students can improve their scores and speed up their work, ensuring they are fully prepared.

LESSON 1 Finding the Place Value with Whole Numbers and Decimals

In this exercise you'll be asked to identify the value of a specific digit within a number. It's wise to be careful with these questions as, while they are relatively straightforward, they can be easy to slip up on. Let's have a look at some examples.

Example 1

In the number 3,079, what value is the 7?

If you're confident about place values, you'll know immediately that the answer is 70. If you're not, draw a place value table on a piece of scrap paper and write the numbers on it like this:

Thousands 1,000	Hundreds 100	Tens 10	Units 1	Decimal point .	tenths $\frac{1}{10}$	hundredths $\frac{1}{100}$	thousandths $\frac{1}{1000}$
3	0	7	9	.			

Note how the number is written in the grid. If a number does not have a decimal point then its last digit (in this case the 9) goes in the units column and the others go in the columns on the left of that, in order. Now when you look at the digit 7 you can see that it's in the 'Tens' column – so it's worth 7 tens. This is the same as <u>70</u>, so that is the answer you would mark on your answer sheet.

Example 2

In the number 34.78, what value is the 7?

Thousands 1,000	Hundreds 100	Tens 10	Units 1	Decimal point .	tenths $\frac{1}{10}$	hundredths $\frac{1}{100}$	thousandths $\frac{1}{1000}$
		3	4	.	7	8	

To place numbers with decimal points correctly on a place value grid, first put the decimal point in the correct place and then place the digits starting with those closest to it. Remember you can only have one digit in each column. Do this correctly and you'll get them in the right place every time.

In the example above, the 7 is now in the 'tenths' column so its place value is a fraction. It could be written as 0.7, or $\frac{7}{10}$ but not as 7 tens or 70, so watch out for these. Check your answer grid carefully for how the number should be written. The answer in this instance is <u>7 tenths</u>.

HELPFUL HINTS

Draw one large place value chart so that you can fit all your workings on it, without having to redraw it for each question. Also make sure your chart goes up to tens and hundreds of thousands for larger numbers.

LESSON 1 PART 1

My Time

My Score

Now look at the questions below. Try to do them quickly and mark your answers in the corresponding grids on the opposite page. You have 20 minutes to complete this task. Write the time you took and your score in the boxes above once you've finished.

1 In the number 2,038, what value is the 2?

2 In the number 12,104, what value is the 4?

3 In the number 135,027, what value is the 5?

4 In the number 73.6, what value is the 6?

5 In the number 23.04, what value is the 4?

6 In the number 261.08, what value is the 1?

7 In the number 4,032.6, what value is the 6?

8 In the number 2,867,034, what value is the 8?

9 In the number 6,407,821, what value is the 6?

10 In the number 450.358, what value is the 8?

LESSON 1 PART 1: ANSWER SHEET

Mark your answer by putting a horizontal line in 1 of the boxes, as in the examples below.

Example 1:

7 tenths ☐
7 ☐
70 ☐ (marked)
700 ☐
7,000 ☐

Example 2:

7 hundredths ☐
7 tenths ☐ (marked)
7 ☐
70 ☐
700 ☐

1

2 ☐
20 ☐
200 ☐
2,000 ☐
20,000 ☐

2

400 ☐
40 ☐
4 tenths ☐
4 ☐
4,000 ☐

3

5 million ☐
500,000 ☐
50 ☐
5 hundredths ☐
5,000 ☐

4

60 ☐
6 tenths ☐
6 hundredths ☐
600 ☐
6,000 ☐

5

400 ☐
40 ☐
4 ☐
4,000 ☐
4 hundredths ☐

6

1 tenth ☐
1 hundredth ☐
10 ☐
1 ☐
100 ☐

7

600 ☐
6 million ☐
60 ☐
6 tenths ☐
6 hundredths ☐

8

8,000 ☐
8 million ☐
80,000 ☐
800,000 ☐
800 ☐

9

6 million ☐
60 ☐
6 hundredths ☐
60,000 ☐
6,000 ☐

10

8 tenths ☐
8 hundredths ☐
8 thousandths ☐
8 thousand ☐
8 hundred ☐

How Did You Do? Let's Find Out!

Here are the correct answers. You may mark your answers to these questions yourself.

1. 2,000
2. 4
3. 5,000
4. 6 tenths
5. 4 hundredths
6. 1
7. 6 tenths
8. 800,000
9. 6 million
10. 8 thousandths

If you scored 9 or 10 out of 10

I consider these questions pretty straightforward so this is a good score. As long as you're careful, you should do well on these questions, but do check which answers you got wrong. Then move on to the next set of questions.

If you scored 7 to 8 out of 10

This score is okay, but you should aim to score higher. Check which answers you got wrong, and make sure you understand how to work out the answer before you move on. Also check that you didn't make a mistake when marking your answers on the answer grid.

If you scored fewer than 7 out of 10

This is quite a low score so let's work really hard to improve. Read the following advice to help you before you move on to the next set of questions.

➪ Do you know all your place value numbers in written and number form? Make sure you learn these or you might well continue to struggle with other questions. See the further hint below for more on this.

Further hint

Numbers can be represented in word or number form. Occasionally there may even be a mix of the two. The table below shows you how different numbers may be represented.

Make careful note of the difference between tens and tenths, hundreds and hundredths etc.

Additionally, some numbers, such as fractions, can be represented in decimal or percentage form. The table below shows some common ones to look out for.

Word form	Number form	Mixed
nine thousandths	$\frac{9}{1000}$	9 thousandths
sixty-three hundredths	$\frac{63}{100}$	63 hundredths
seven tenths	$\frac{7}{10}$	7 tenths
thirty	30	3 tens
two hundred	200	2 hundred
five thousand	5,000	5 thousand

Word form	Fraction	Decimal	Percent
one thousandth	$\frac{1}{1000}$	0.001	0.1%
one hundredth	$\frac{1}{100}$	0.01	1%
one tenth	$\frac{1}{10}$	0.1	10%
one fifth	$\frac{1}{5}$	0.2	20%
one quarter	$\frac{1}{4}$	0.25	25%
two fifths	$\frac{2}{5}$	0.4	40%
one half	$\frac{1}{2}$	0.5	50%
three fifths	$\frac{3}{5}$	0.6	60%
three quarters	$\frac{3}{4}$	0.75	75%
four fifths	$\frac{4}{5}$	0.8	80%

LESSON 1 PART 2

My Time

My Score

Now let's try some more. You have 20 minutes to complete these.

Mark your answers on the corresponding grids on the opposite page. Remember you'll need to get an adult to mark these ones for you. Write the time you took and your score in the boxes above once you've finished.

1. In the number 40,056, what value is the 4?
2. In the number 32.09, what value is the 9?
3. In the number 347.8, what value is the 3?
4. In the number 600.58, what value is the 8?
5. In the number 24,869.3, what value is the 3?
6. In the number 501,607, what value is the 5?
7. In the number 37.094, what value is the 4?
8. In the number 2,159,034, what value is the 1?
9. In the number 405,076.3, what value is the 3?
10. In the number 42.96, what value is the 6?

LESSON 1 PART 2: ANSWER SHEET

Mark your answer by putting a horizontal line in 1 of the boxes, as in the examples below.

Example 1:

- 7 tenths
- 7
- 70 (marked)
- 700
- 7,000

Example 2:

- 7 hundredths
- 7 tenths (marked)
- 7
- 70
- 700

1
- 40
- 400,000
- 4
- 40,000
- 4 tenths

2
- 900
- 9
- 90
- 9 hundredths
- 9 tenths

3
- 3 hundredths
- 30
- 300
- 3 tenths
- 3,000

4
- 80
- 8
- 800
- 8 hundredths
- 8 thousand

5
- 3 hundred
- 3 thousand
- thirty
- 3 hundredths
- 3 tenths

6
- 5 million
- 500,000
- 50,000
- 5,000
- 5 hundredths

7
- 4 thousand
- 4 hundred
- forty
- 4 thousandths
- 4 hundredths

8
- 100
- 100,000
- 1
- 1,000
- 1 thousandth

9
- thirty
- 3 tenths
- 300
- 3,000
- 3 hundredths

10
- 600
- 60
- 6 tenths
- 6 hundredths
- 6,000

LESSON 2 Calculating Fractions of a Whole Number

The two parts of a fraction are: $\dfrac{\textbf{numerator}}{\textbf{denominator}}$

Remember these names as they'll be referred to later on.

In this exercise you're given an amount and asked to calculate what a particular fraction or part of that amount is. To do this you'll need to learn the following method:

To find the fraction of a whole number you first divide the number by the denominator. Then multiply the answer by the numerator. Here's an example.

Example

In a bakery $2/5$ of 40 pies have cherries. How many pies is this?

First: $40 \div 5 = 8$ $(40 \div \text{denominator} = 8)$

Then: $8 \times 2 = 16$ $(8 \times \text{numerator} = 16)$

So 16 pies have cherries.

HELPFUL HINTS

- When answering these types of questions, do read them carefully. In the question above, I could have asked you how many pies didn't have cherries. In this case, since 16 pies had cherries and there were 40 pies in total, I would simply take 16 from 40 to get my answer 24. This answer is also given as a choice on the grid just to keep you on your toes, so pay attention – don't get caught out!
- Work out the problems on paper first, then mark your answer on the multiple choice grid.
- Remember to learn the words denominator and numerator and which is which – they come up all the time in fractions!

LESSON 2 PART 1

My Time

My Score

Now look at the questions below. Work them out on scrap paper first and then mark your answers on the sheet on the opposite page. You have 20 minutes to complete this task. Write the time you took and your score in the boxes above once you've finished.

1. In a factory $\frac{2}{3}$ of 66 cars are yellow. How many is this?
2. Mr Botts has 24 children in his year 4 class, of whom $\frac{3}{8}$ forget their homework. How many remember it?
3. A bookshop sells 640 books each week. Of these $\frac{3}{5}$ are fiction. How many fiction books are sold each week?
4. In a garden of 36 trees, $\frac{1}{12}$ are elms. How many trees are not elms?
5. In a jeweller's shop, there are 72 precious stones, of which $\frac{1}{6}$ are rubies and $\frac{3}{6}$ are diamonds. How many stones are rubies?
6. If $\frac{2}{7}$ of a farm's animals are goats and there are 490 animals on the farm, how many goats are there?
7. In a local post office, 540 letters are posted each day. Of these $\frac{7}{9}$ are first class. How many letters is this?
8. In a vegetable patch of 88 crops, $\frac{3}{11}$ are potatoes, $\frac{5}{11}$ are beans and the rest are peas. How many peas are there?
9. In a magazine of 48 pages, 12 pages are for advertising; what fraction of the magazine pages would this be?
10. In a choir of 42 children, 14 children sing alto. What fraction of the choir would this be?

LESSON 2 PART 1: ANSWER SHEET

Mark your answer by putting a horizontal line in 1 of the boxes, as in the example below.

Example:

20
16
10
8
40

1

68
33
22
44
66

2

16
24
3
9
15

3

64
21
128
256
384

4

24
12
3
33
4

5

12
48
36
60
24

6

14
70
140
350
420

7

60
420
480
42
48

8

11
8
64
24
40

9

1 quarter
1 eighth
1 twelfth
1 half
1 third

10

1 half
1 third
1 quarter
1 fifth
1 sixth

How Did You Do? Let's Find Out!

Here are the correct answers. You may mark your answers to these questions yourself.

1 44

2 15

3 384

4 33

5 12

6 140

7 420

8 24

9 1 quarter

10 1 third

If you scored 8 or more out of 10

These questions can be quite tricky so this is a good score. If you scored 8 or 9, check where you went wrong. Look at the further hint on the next page before you move on to the next set of questions.

If you scored 5 to 7 out of 10

Check which answers you got wrong, and make sure you understand how to work out the answer before you move on. Also, check that you didn't make a mistake when marking your answers on the answer sheet. Read the further hint below and then move on to the next set of questions.

If you scored fewer than 5 out of 10

These questions can be tricky but you do have to improve your score. Try to find out where you went wrong before you move on to the next set of questions.

- ➪ Do you understand what to do? If not, read the instructions and practise the method again with an adult to make sure you know how to calculate the correct answer.

- ➪ Did you mark the wrong answers on the answer sheet? This is a common mistake. Pay close attention to your marking, making sure you put the mark next to the right answer. If you do this you won't get the answers wrong simply because of a marking error.

- ➪ Do you remember which number is the denominator and which is the numerator? Check this before you move on.

Further hint

Did you notice that the last two questions were in a slightly different format to the first 8 questions? Don't panic when you see these – both questions give a whole number that is in fact a fraction of the total amount. You simply need to divide the total amount by the whole number. This answer will be the denominator of your fraction. The numerator in such answers is always 1. Look at my working below.

Example

In a magazine of 48 pages, 12 pages are for advertising.
What fraction of the magazine pages would this be?

You must find out what fraction 12 is of 48. To do this you divide 48 by 12, which is equal to 4. So 4 becomes the denominator.

Your fraction answer would therefore be $\frac{1}{4}$.

LESSON 2 PART 2

My Time

My Score

Now let's try some more. Work out the answers on some scrap paper and then mark your answers on the sheet on the opposite page. You have 20 minutes to complete this task. Remember an adult needs to mark these for you. Write the time you took and your score in the boxes above once you've finished.

1 In a factory, $\frac{1}{3}$ of 120 boxes contain toys. How many boxes contain toys?

2 Out of a total of 300 days, $\frac{3}{10}$ are holidays. How many are work days?

3 A computer shop sells 108 items each week. Of these $\frac{4}{9}$ are printers. How many printers are sold each week?

4 In a museum containing 56 pictures, $\frac{5}{8}$ are modern art. How many pictures are not modern art?

5 In a clothing store, of 1,860 clothes $\frac{1}{6}$ are blouses and $\frac{2}{6}$ are jumpers. How many jumpers are there?

6 A zoo has a total of 458 animals. Of these $\frac{1}{2}$ are mammals. How many are not mammals?

7 In a local office, 63 telephone calls are answered each day. Of these $\frac{5}{9}$ are emergencies. How many calls are emergencies?

8 In a farm shop selling 144 items, $\frac{3}{12}$ are chickens, $\frac{5}{12}$ are turnips and the rest are pumpkins. How many pumpkins are there?

9 In a newspaper of 60 pages, 12 pages are for advertising. What fraction of the magazine would represent this?

10 In a game show audience of 480, 80 people win prizes. What fraction of the audience is this?

LESSON 2 PART 2: ANSWER SHEET

Mark your answer by putting a horizontal line in 1 of the boxes, as in the example below.

Example:

20 ▭
16 ▬
10 ▭
8 ▭
40 ▭

1
4 ▭
40 ▭
15 ▭
80 ▭
12 ▭

2
90 ▭
100 ▭
30 ▭
210 ▭
60 ▭

3
12 ▭
48 ▭
36 ▭
27 ▭
60 ▭

4
7 ▭
35 ▭
42 ▭
48 ▭
21 ▭

5
310 ▭
620 ▭
930 ▭
31 ▭
62 ▭

6
229 ▭
254 ▭
225 ▭
227 ▭
228 ▭

7
7 ▭
35 ▭
28 ▭
45 ▭
54 ▭

8
12 ▭
36 ▭
60 ▭
96 ▭
48 ▭

9
1 half ▭
1 third ▭
1 quarter ▭
1 fifth ▭
1 sixth ▭

10
1 half ▭
1 third ▭
1 quarter ▭
1 fifth ▭
1 sixth ▭

LESSON 3 Finding the Whole Number From a Fraction

These questions are easy to confuse with those you've just tackled in lesson 2, so be very careful. Always read the question a second time to ensure that you're doing the right thing.

In this exercise you're given a fraction and what it is worth as a number. You then have to find out what the original total amount was. You do this by using the opposite method to that used in lesson 2. This time you're going to divide the number you have by the numerator and then multiply the answer by the denominator.

Let's look at an example to see how it works. (I am going to use the same example as lesson 2 in order to show you the difference.)

Example

In a bakery $^2/_5$ of the pies have cherries. If 16 pies have cherries, how many pies were baked in total?

So you know that there are 16 pies with cherries and that $16 = {}^2/_5$ of the total number that were baked.

You need to find how many pies are equal to $^1/_5$ of the whole amount. You do this by dividing 16 by the numerator. $16 \div 2 = 8$. So $8 = {}^1/_5$.

To find the total amount you must multiply your answer by the denominator.

So $8 \times 5 = 40$. Therefore 40 pies were baked originally.

HELPFUL HINTS

- Read the question carefully. The question types shown in lessons 2 and 3 are easy to mix up, so be on your guard.
- If you find that your answer is not a whole number, you might have done the wrong calculation. Go back and read the question again.
- Think about your answer. Does it make sense? Is it reasonable or is it too big or small? If it doesn't look right, check that you've done the right calculation.

LESSON 3 PART 1

My Time	My Score

Now look at the questions below. Work them out on some scrap paper and then mark your answers on the sheet on the opposite page. You have 20 minutes to complete this task. Write the time you took and your score in the boxes above once you've finished.

1 In a factory 30 boxes contain eggs. If this is $^2/_3$ of the total, then, how many boxes are there all together?

2 A travel agent sold 350 skiing holidays. If this is $^7/_{10}$ of the total, how many holidays were sold in all?

3 A computer shop sold 16 computers, which represented $^4/_5$ of its total sales. How many did it sell in total?

4 A total of 210 children watched a film. If this was $^3/_7$ of the audience, how many people were there in all?

5 If a petrol tank holds 42 litres when it's $^3/_4$ full, how much more petrol does it need to fill it up?

6 If a zoo feeds 129 animals meat and this represents $^3/_5$ of the animals, how many animals are there in the zoo in total?

7 Only 12 calls are unanswered in an office and this is $^1/_6$ of the total. How many calls are answered?

8 If a swimming pool contains 140 gallons of water when it is a quarter full, how much water can it hold when it is full?

9 If I am one-third of the way through a book when I've read 73 pages, how many pages does the book have?

10 In a game Dillon has two-thirds of his opponent's score when he reaches 28 points. How many points does his opponent have?

LESSON 3 PART 1: ANSWER SHEET

Mark your answer by putting a horizontal line in 1 of the boxes, as in the example below.

Example:

10 ▭
40 ▬
13 ▭
45 ▭
32 ▭

1	2	3	4
90 ▭	500 ▭	20 ▭	630 ▭
60 ▭	3,500 ▭	21 ▭	220 ▭
20 ▭	70 ▭	25 ▭	490 ▭
45 ▭	357 ▭	64 ▭	2,100 ▭
36 ▭	35 ▭	80 ▭	231 ▭

5	6	7	8
56 litres ▭	43 ▭	18 ▭	35 gallons ▭
12 litres ▭	144 ▭	60 ▭	175 gallons ▭
10 litres ▭	387 ▭	72 ▭	420 gallons ▭
30 litres ▭	215 ▭	2 ▭	560 gallons ▭
14 litres ▭	645 ▭	19 ▭	700 gallons ▭

9	10
24 pages ▭	14 ▭
97 pages ▭	42 ▭
76 pages ▭	34 ▭
219 pages ▭	56 ▭
209 pages ▭	84 ▭

How Did You Do? Let's Find Out!

Here are the correct answers. You may mark your answers to these questions yourself.

1 45

2 500

3 20

4 490

5 14 litres

6 215

7 60

8 560 gallons

9 219 pages

10 42

If you scored 8 or more out of 10

Well done, this is a good result. If you scored 8 or 9, check where you went wrong. Look at the further hint on the next page before you move on to the next set of questions.

If you scored 5 to 7 out of 10

Let's work to improve this score. Check which answers you got wrong and make sure you understand how to work out the answer before you move on. Also, check that you didn't make a mistake when marking your answers on the answer sheet. Read the further hint on the next page and then move on to the next set of questions.

If you scored fewer than 5 out of 10

Fewer than 5 is quite low so you'll need to practise these. Try to understand where you went wrong before you move on to the next set of questions.

- Do you understand what to do? If not, read the instructions and practise the method again with an adult to make sure you know how to calculate the correct answer.

- Double check and make sure you don't confuse this question with the type you saw in lesson 2.

- Do you remember which number is the denominator and which is the numerator? As with the last lesson, you need to be certain of these before you move on to the next lesson.

Further hint

Did you notice something different in question 5? Instead of simply asking you to work out the original total, I asked you to tell me how much more was needed to get to that total. Read these questions carefully – the maths isn't any more difficult but it is easy to get caught out. First, work out the total, then simply find the difference between the total and what you already have. You can see this in the example below.

Example

If a petrol tank holds 42 litres when it is three-quarters full, how much more petrol does it need to fill it up?

You begin by following the usual steps. You know that $3/4$ equals 42 litres so you divide 42 by the numerator 3 to find $1/4$.

$42 \div 3 = 14$.

Now multiply this by the denominator 4 to find the total.

$14 \times 4 = 56$.

If you already have 42 litres, how many more litres do you need to make it up to 56 litres? That's simple:

$56 - 42 = \underline{14}$ litres.

So that's your answer.

LESSON 3 PART 2

My Time

My Score

Now let's try some more. Work these questions out on some scrap paper and then mark your answers on the opposite page. You have 20 minutes to complete this task. Write the time you took and your score in the boxes above once you've finished. Remember an adult needs to mark these for you.

1 In a factory 12 people are sick. If this is $2/3$ of the workforce, how many people does the factory employ?

2 If 39 books were returned to the library, and that is $3/5$ of the daily total, what is the daily total?

3 A pet shop sold 12 rabbits which represented $4/10$ of its total sales. How many did it sell in total?

4 An aquarium has 35 clown fish which are $7/11$ of the total. How many fish are there in all?

5 If a bath tub holds 33 litres of water when it is $3/8$ full, how much more water does it need to fill it up?

6 If a cinema holds 360 people when it is $6/7$ full, how many people can it hold in total?

7 Only 15 letters were undelivered by a courier company and this is $3/20$ of the total letters. How many letters were delivered?

8 If a washing machine contains 3,200ml of water when it is a quarter full, how much water can it hold when it is full?

9 If I am two-fifths of the way through a book when I have read 84 pages, how many pages does the book have?

10 Two-thirds of telephone calls made from a house last more than 30 minutes. If this is 88 calls, how many do not last more than 30 minutes?

LESSON 3 PART 2: ANSWER SHEET

Mark your answer by putting a horizontal line in 1 of the boxes, as in the example below.

Example:

Example
10 ▭
40 ▬
13 ▭
45 ▭
32 ▭

1	2	3	4
14 ▭	13 ▭	16 ▭	42 ▭
15 ▭	65 ▭	40 ▭	46 ▭
18 ▭	54 ▭	30 ▭	63 ▭
8 ▭	15 ▭	52 ▭	112 ▭
6 ▭	24 ▭	28 ▭	55 ▭

5	6	7	8
57 litres ▭	60 ▭	85 ▭	3,204ml ▭
11 litres ▭	420 ▭	60 ▭	7,200ml ▭
44 litres ▭	402 ▭	65 ▭	3,600ml ▭
55 litres ▭	4,200 ▭	38 ▭	12,800ml ▭
49 litres ▭	4,020 ▭	100 ▭	1,280ml ▭

9	10
210 pages ▭	44 ▭
168 pages ▭	94 ▭
420 pages ▭	132 ▭
42 pages ▭	60 ▭
94 pages ▭	118 ▭

LESSON 4 Simplifying Fractions

In this exercise, first you'll need to work out what the fraction is in its raw form. Then you'll simplify it to get the answer on the answer grid.

To simplify a fraction, you'll need to list the factors of both the numerator and the denominator.

A factor is any number which divides into another number.

Next, check which one or more of the factors appear in both lists. Choose the biggest of these common factors and divide both parts of your fraction by it. This will give you your fraction in its simplest form. Let's look at an example.

Example

Boris scores 15 out of 20 in a spelling test. Write his score as a fraction in its lowest terms and then list all the factors for both the numerator and the denominator.

15 factors: 1, 3, 5, 15 (In other words 15 is divisible by 1, 3, 5 and 15)
20 factors: 1, 2, 4, 5, 10, 20 (20 is divisible by 1, 2, 4, 5, 10 and 20)

Look at the lists of factors: you can see that the numbers 1 and 5 appear in both sets. You want the biggest of these, which is often called the 'greatest common factor'.

The greatest common factor in this example is 5.

Now divide your numerator and denominator by 5.

$$\frac{15 \div 5}{20 \div 5} = \frac{3}{4}$$

So the fraction in its simplest form is $\frac{3}{4}$.

HELPFUL HINTS

- Note that when I say 'simplify', 'simplest form', 'reduce' or 'lowest terms', they all mean the same thing!
- Not all fractions can be simplified so make sure you find a common factor before you start trying.

LESSON 4 PART 1

My Time

My Score

Now look at the questions below. Work them out on a separate piece of paper and then mark your answers on the answer sheet. You have 20 minutes to complete this task. Write the time you took and your score in the boxes above once you've finished.

1. Imran has a box of 8 chocolates; if he eats 2 of them, what fraction remains?

2. Alice scored 30 out of 40 on a maths test. Write this as a fraction in its simplest form.

3. In a class of 32 children, 20 bring a packed lunch. What fraction of the class does not?

4. A factory produces 600 cars each week. If 180 of these are silver, write this as a fraction in its lowest terms.

5. If a pizza is split into 12 equal pieces and four people share it equally, what fraction of the pizza does each person get?

6. If a cinema holds 840 people and only 240 turned up for the film, what fraction of seats remained empty?

7. Brenda sent invites for a party. Of her 25 friends, only 15 could make it; what fraction is this?

8. Of 56 books returned to a library in 1 day, 21 were overdue. What fraction represents this?

9. Faiza has read 24 pages of a book containing a total of 168 pages. What fraction of the book is this?

10. A primary school football team won 6 out of its 24 matches in a season. What fraction is this in its lowest terms?

LESSON 4 PART 1: ANSWER SHEET

Mark your answer by putting a horizontal line in 1 of the boxes as in the example below.

Example:

- 1/20
- 5/20
- 3/4 ▬
- 4/5
- 5/6

1
- 1/4
- 2/4
- 3/4
- 4/8
- 2/8

2
- 10/40
- 10/30
- 3/3
- 3/4
- 3/10

3
- 10/16
- 5/8
- 3/8
- 6/32
- 6/8

4
- 3/10
- 18/60
- 90/300
- 2/30
- 3/6

5
- 4/12
- 1/12
- 1/3
- 1/4
- 1/6

6
- 3/8
- 5/7
- 3/5
- 4/5
- 1/6

7
- 15/23
- 5/7
- 3/7
- 4/9
- 3/5

8
- 10/28
- 14/27
- 3/8
- 2/7
- 4/9

9
- 1/3
- 1/4
- 1/5
- 1/6
- 1/7

10
- 3/8
- 1/5
- 1/4
- 2/7
- 5/9

How Did You Do? Let's Find Out!

Here are the correct answers. You may mark your answers to these questions yourself.

1 $^3/_4$

2 $^3/_4$

3 $^3/_8$

4 $^3/_{10}$

5 $^1/_4$

6 $^5/_7$

7 $^3/_5$

8 $^3/_8$

9 $^1/_7$

10 $^1/_4$

If you scored 8 or more out of 10

These questions can be quite tricky so this is a good score. Look at the further hint on the next page before you move on to the next set of questions.

If you scored 5 to 7 out of 10

This score is okay, but you need to score higher. Check which answers you got wrong and make sure you understand how to work out the answer before you move on. Check that you didn't make a mistake when marking your answers on the answer grid.

If you scored fewer than 5 out of 10

This score is quite low so you'll need to improve, which you can do with a bit more practice. Read the following advice to help you improve before you move on to the next set of questions.

➪ Do you understand what to do? If not, read the instructions and practise the method again with an adult to make sure you know how to calculate the correct answer.

➪ Did you lose your place or put the wrong answer on the answer grid? This is a common mistake. Try to keep your place so you don't get questions wrong simply because of a marking error.

➪ Did you remember to simplify your answer? Have another look and try to understand where you went wrong.

Further hint

Did you notice something tricky about questions 4 and 6? In these cases it would be far too time consuming to find all the factors of numbers such as 180 and 600! Instead you need to do something far smarter.

First, look at how each number ends. They both end with a 0 which tells you that both numbers can be divided by 10. This should bring both down to a much more reasonable number to deal with.

Example 1

$$\frac{180 \div 10}{600 \div 10} = \frac{18}{60}$$

Now it should be easier to find the common factor for these numbers.

Additionally, if you notice in fractions with larger numbers that both numbers are even you can divide both by 2 (halve them) to make it easier to find the factors.

Example 2

$$\frac{18 \div 2}{60 \div 2} = \frac{9}{30}$$

This fraction still isn't in its lowest terms despite using the shortcut so make sure you make it even smaller.

The answer to both examples is $\frac{3}{10}$.

LESSON 4 PART 2

My Time

My Score

Now look at the questions below. Work them out on some scrap paper and then mark your answers on the opposite page. You have 20 minutes to complete this task. Write the time you took and your score in the boxes above once you've finished. Remember an adult needs to mark these for you.

1 Rachel and Gordon calculate that they saw 36 out of a possible 62 animals at the zoo. What fraction is this in its simplest form?

2 Only 22 out of 32 students passed their driving test. What fraction didn't succeed?

3 In a restaurant, the manager calculates that 14 tables out of 20 are being used. What fraction are not being used?

4 A supermarket sold 240 cartons of skimmed milk and 360 cartons of full cream milk. Of all the milk sold, what fraction was skimmed milk?

5 In a competition 4 people win £28 and split it equally. What fraction of the money does each person win?

6 In a class of 26 children, 6 forgot their swimming kit. What fraction is this?

7 Carly drank 150ml of a 400ml can of drink. What fraction is this?

8 Drew calculates that he spent 20 days of November in school. What fraction of November did he not spend in school?

9 Penny has read 42 pages of a book containing a total of 210 pages. What fraction of the book remains for her to read?

10 A primary school football team won 6 and drew 7 of its 26 matches in a season. What fraction did it lose?

LESSON 4 PART 2: ANSWER SHEET

Mark your answer by putting a horizontal line in 1 of the boxes, as in the example below.

Example:

- 1/20 ☐
- 5/20 ☐
- 3/4 ⊟
- 4/5 ☐
- 5/6 ☐

1	2	3	4	5
10/31 ☐	11/16 ☐	7/10 ☐	24/36 ☐	4/7 ☐
18/31 ☐	10/16 ☐	14/20 ☐	2/3 ☐	7/28 ☐
24/62 ☐	22/32 ☐	6/10 ☐	2/5 ☐	11/28 ☐
12/31 ☐	5/16 ☐	3/5 ☐	3/5 ☐	7/11 ☐
24/31 ☐	6/16 ☐	3/10 ☐	5/12 ☐	1/4 ☐

6	7	8	9	10
20/26 ☐	15/35 ☐	1/3 ☐	1/5 ☐	6/26 ☐
10/13 ☐	35/40 ☐	10/20 ☐	2/5 ☐	7/26 ☐
6/13 ☐	3/15 ☐	10/31 ☐	3/5 ☐	6/13 ☐
3/13 ☐	8/15 ☐	2/3 ☐	4/5 ☐	7/13 ☐
6/32 ☐	3/8 ☐	1/6 ☐	5/6 ☐	1/2 ☐

LESSON 5 Adding and Subtracting with Decimals

In this exercise you'll make calculations that are required when you use money or metric measures (see page 124 for a list of metric measures).

The main difficulty with these calculations is deciding where to place the figures when adding or subtracting using the column method. The key is to line up the decimal points first so that they are all in a line from top to bottom. Then you place the figures around them according to where they occur in relation to the decimal point. If the figures don't seem to line up exactly, you can put a 0 in the empty spaces to the right of the decimal point. Only then should you do the calculation.

Let's have a look at an example.

Example

Rosy is sent to the shop by her mother.
She takes a £5 note and the shopping bill comes to £3.47.
How much change should she receive?

You need to <u>exchange and regroup</u> when subtracting; an example of how to do this is shown below. Here you have to subtract £3.47 from £5.00. To do this you must first line the numbers up, like this:

$$\begin{array}{r} £5.00 \\ \underline{-\ £3.47} \end{array}$$

You always begin by subtracting the units but in this case you are unable to do so because there's nothing in the units column.

Instead you need to take a pound from the 5 in the pounds column and break it into tens. It makes 10 tens and when you move it it should look like this.

$$\begin{array}{r} £\,^{4}\not{5}.\,^{1}0\,0 \\ \underline{-\ £\,3.\,4\,7} \end{array}$$

Next you need to take a 10 from the tens column leaving 9 and move it to make 10 units. Finally, you can complete your subtraction like this.

$$\begin{array}{r} £\,^{4}\not{5}.\,^{9}\not{1}\not{0}\,^{1}0 \\ \underline{-\ £\,3.\,4\,7} \\ £\,1.\,5\,3 \end{array}$$

Your final answer is <u>£1.53</u>

Practise using this method until you can do it really well.

LESSON 5 PART 1

My Time

My Score

Now look at the questions below. Work them out on some spare paper and then mark your answers on the corresponding grids. You have 20 minutes to complete this task. Write the time you took and your score in the boxes above once you've finished.

1 A doorway is 2.48m high and the ceiling is 3.1m. What is the difference in height between the doorway and ceiling?

2 A car travels 3.78km in the morning and 0.5km in the afternoon. How far has it travelled in total?

3 If three pieces of string are 0.28m, 1.3m and 2.375m long, what is their combined length?

4 Imran ran 100m in 10.07 seconds. By how many seconds did he beat Gurjeet, who ran 100m in 11.6 seconds?

5 Mr Poole took his wife and 2 children to the Awesome Fairground. He spent £2.75 on each person's entrance fee and then bought a big tub of popcorn for £8.32. How much change did he receive as he gave a £20 note?

6 Allan calculates that his large glass jug contains 2.055 litres of fluid. How much fluid is left if he pours out 640ml?

7 Happy City's population was 1.3 million in 2009. In 2010 it increased by 125,000. What is its new population?

8 A plant measuring 18.3cm in height, grows 87mm in a month. What is its new height?

9 A snail travels 32mm each day for 5 days. How many centimetres has it travelled in total?

10 If Annie took £10 to the local market and returned with £3.28 in change, how much did she spend?

LESSON 5 PART 1: ANSWER SHEET

Mark your answer by putting a horizontal line in 1 of the boxes, as in the example below.

Example:

£8.47
£3.53
£1.53 (marked)
£2.53
£1.63

1	2	3	4
5.58m	2.78km	3.955m	21.67seconds
1.38m	3.28km	3.703m	21.13seconds
2.17m	3.83km	3.855m	1.67seconds
1.18m	4.28km	3.905m	1.53seconds
0.62m	8.78km	1.28m	1.87seconds

5	6	7	8
£19.32	2.695 litres	1.425 million	105.3cm
£39.32	2.615 litres	1.312 million	27cm
£1.32	1.615 litres	1.325 million	19.17cm
£0.68	1.415 litres	2.55 million	888.3cm
£1.68	1.145 litres	1.3125 million	9.6cm

9	10
160cm	£13.28
16cm	£7.28
1.6cm	£6.28
3.7cm	£6.72
37cm	£6.82

How Did You Do? Let's Find Out!

Here are the correct answers. You may mark your answers to these questions yourself.

1. 0.62m
2. 4.28km
3. 3.955m
4. 1.53 seconds
5. £0.68
6. 1.415 litres
7. 1.425 million
8. 27cm
9. 16cm
10. £6.72

If you scored 8 or more out of 10

This is a good score but if you scored 8 or 9, try to improve in the next part of the lesson. Look at the further hint on the next page before you move on to the next set of questions.

If you scored 6 to 7 out of 10

This score is okay, but try to score higher next time. Check which answers you got wrong and make sure you understand how to work out the answer before you move on. Also, check that you didn't make a mistake when marking your answers on the answer sheet. Have a look at the further hint below and then move on to the next set of questions.

If you scored fewer than 6 out of 10

Fewer than 6 is rather low so you need to practise to improve your score. Try to find out why your score was so low before you move on to the next set of questions.

- ⇨ Do you understand what to do? If not, read the instructions and practise the method again with an adult to make sure you know how to calculate the correct answer.
- ⇨ Did you subtract correctly? Did you remember how to exchange and regroup for those questions where it's needed?
- ⇨ Did you line up your decimal points before you subtracted or added?
- ⇨ Did you do the right calculation for the question type – some questions required you to add and others to subtract. You must read the questions carefully.

Further hint

Did you note that some questions required you to do metric conversions? For example if you add 34mm to 6.1cm, the answer is 9.5cm. To add 34mm to 6.1cm you first convert both into the same metric units. 34mm÷10=3.4cm. Now you can add them in the usual way

$$\begin{array}{r} 3.4\text{cm} \\ \underline{+\ 6.1\text{cm}} \\ 9.5\text{cm} \end{array}$$

You must know all your metric conversions so if you don't, learn the ones on page 124 before you move on.

LESSON 5 PART 2

My Time

My Score

Now let's try some more. Work these questions out on scrap paper and then mark your answers on the opposite page. You have 20 minutes to complete this task. Watch out for those metric conversions and remember, an adult needs to mark this set of questions. Write the time you took and your score in the boxes above once you've finished.

1 A television costs £109.99 but is reduced by £15.49 in the sale. What is its new price?

2 Road repairers re-lay 13.74 miles of road in 1 week and 14.39 miles the next. How much road have they repaired in total?

3 How much faster was the skier who completed the course in 28.92 seconds than the one who completed it in 30.11 seconds?

4 Mr Barnes calculated that his new car was 88cm longer than his old one. If his old one was 3.84m long how long is his new car?

5 How much change will Thelma get if she uses a £10 note to buy a lemon for 49p, an avocado for £1.09 and a chicken for £4.99?

6 Karl walked 2.309km for charity. How far short of two and a half kilometres was he?

7 Bags on Quick Airlines must not exceed 5kg in weight. If Mr Jones has a bag weighing 4,039g, how many grams is it under this weight?

8 Colin measures 1.57m and his sister is 18cm shorter. How tall is she?

9 If 453ml of water is spilled from a jug holding 1.5 litres, how much water is still left in the jug?

10 Charvis returns from the shop and explains that he spent £6.49. If he has £3.42 in his pocket, how much money did he take to the shop?

LESSON 5 PART 2: ANSWER SHEET

Mark your answer by putting a horizontal line in 1 of the boxes, as in the example below.

Example:

£8.47 ☐
£3.53 ☐
£1.53 ⊟
£2.53 ☐
£1.63 ☐

1

£94.50 ☐
£125.48 ☐
£104.50 ☐
£95.40 ☐
£96.50 ☐

2

1.45 miles ☐
27.13 miles ☐
0.65 miles ☐
28.13 miles ☐
28.04 miles ☐

3

58.81 seconds ☐
2.81 seconds ☐
1.81 seconds ☐
2.19 seconds ☐
1.19 seconds ☐

4

3.04m ☐
4.62m ☐
4.72m ☐
4.82m ☐
3.72m ☐

5

£6.57 ☐
£3.51 ☐
£16.57 ☐
£3.53 ☐
£3.43 ☐

6

4.809km ☐
0.809km ☐
0.201km ☐
0.191km ☐
0.181km ☐

7

9,039g ☐
4,539g ☐
1,039g ☐
961g ☐
1,061g ☐

8

1.75m ☐
1.41m ☐
1.39m ☐
1.31m ☐
1.30m ☐

9

1.953 litres ☐
1.153 litres ☐
1.503 litres ☐
1.047 litres ☐
1.147 litres ☐

10

£3.07 ☐
£3.87 ☐
£9.81 ☐
£9.91 ☐
£10.00 ☐

LESSON 6 Turning Fractions Into Decimals and Percentages

Percentage means 'out of 100'.

In this exercise you'll be given a fraction and asked to convert it into a percentage. To do this, you can use the factors of 100. These are the numbers by which you can divide 100 and get a whole number. You must know these so here they are for you to learn.

Factors of 100: 1, 2, 4, 5, 10, 20, 25, 50, 100.

It's important to understand not only these types of question but also the link between percentages, fractions and decimals. This is a key part of mathematics.

Here's an example to see how you can use these factors.

Example

Hisham scored 18 out of 25 in a maths test. What percentage is this?

First write Hisham's score out as a fraction: $^{18}/_{25}$

Because percentage means out of 100, you should then express this fraction with 100 as its denominator. To turn 25ths into 100ths you need to multiply them by 4. Next, you must also do this to the numerator.

Remember, you must always do the same to the numerator as you do to the denominator. So if you multiply the denominator by 4 to get 100, you must also multiply the numerator by 4:

$$\frac{18 \times 4}{25 \times 4} = \frac{72}{100}$$

$^{72}/_{100}$ as a percentage is 72%. This is the answer you mark on your grid.

You can go one step further and also turn a percentage into a decimal. All you have to do is write out your new fraction, which is 72 hundredths, on your place value chart.

units	decimal point	tenths	hundredths
0	.	7	2

So written as a decimal, 72% is 0.72

LESSON 6 PART 1

My Time

My Score

Now look at the questions below. Do your workings on some scrap paper and then mark your answers on the opposite page. You have 20 minutes to complete this task. Write the time you took and your score in the boxes above once you've finished.

1. Ten out of 20 children in a class walk to school. What percentage is this?
2. Kelly began the year with 10 new pens in her pencil box. If 7 have run out of ink, what percentage will still work?
3. Romily calculates that her spelling test score was worth 85%. If the test was out of 20, what did she score?
4. Harriet has a chocolate bar made up of 20 segments. Her brother Roman ate 7 segments. What percentage of the bar did he eat?
5. If a coach has 50 seats and there are people sitting on 43 of them, what percentage of seats is empty?
6. The local council carried out a survey. Out of 100 people, 58 said they liked the colour of the buses. What percentage is this?
7. If I have £1 in my pocket and I give my brother 78% of this, how much money will I have left?
8. If 92% of houses in a street have central heating and this represents 23 houses, how many houses are there in the street in total?
9. Four-fifths of students at a school always complete their homework on time. What percentage of the school students is this?
10. If three-quarters of a football team prefer pepperoni on their pizza and the rest prefer cheese, what percentage prefers cheese?

LESSON 6 PART 1: ANSWER SHEET

Mark your answer by putting a horizontal line in 1 of the boxes, as in the example below.

Example:

50% ▭
25% ▭
72% ▬
80% ▭
18% ▭

1
10% ▭
20% ▭
5% ▭
50% ▭
100% ▭

2
7% ▭
3% ▭
30% ▭
70% ▭
10% ▭

3
15 ▭
16 ▭
17 ▭
18 ▭
19 ▭

4
20% ▭
7% ▭
13% ▭
35% ▭
65% ▭

5
50% ▭
43% ▭
86% ▭
14% ▭
57% ▭

6
58% ▭
42% ▭
100% ▭
158% ▭
142% ▭

7
£0.78 ▭
£0.22 ▭
£0.10 ▭
£2.20 ▭
£7.80 ▭

8
21 ▭
22 ▭
23 ▭
24 ▭
25 ▭

9
80% ▭
40% ▭
50% ▭
4% ▭
20% ▭

10
12% ▭
3% ▭
25% ▭
75% ▭
4% ▭

How Did You Do? Let's Find Out!

Here are the correct answers. You may mark your answers to these questions yourself.

1 50%

2 30%

3 17

4 35%

5 14%

6 58%

7 £0.22

8 25

9 80%

10 25%

If you scored 8 or more out of 10

This is a good score, but if you scored 8 or 9, try to improve in the next part of the lesson. Check where you went wrong and look at the further hints on the next page before you move on to the next set of questions.

If you scored 6 to 7 out of 10

This score is ok, but check which answers you got wrong and make sure you understand how to work out the answer before you move on. Make sure you didn't make a mistake when marking your answers on the answer sheet. Read the further hints on the next page and then move on to the next set of questions.

If you scored fewer than 6 out of 10

Read the following advice to help you improve your score before you move on to the next set of questions.

- Do you understand what to do? If not, get an adult to go over the instructions with you again. Then have a look at any questions you got wrong and try to understand why your answers are incorrect.
- Make sure you keep your place on the answer sheet and check you have filled in the correct answer each time.
- Do you know the factors of 100 well enough? Make sure that you do and then look at the further hints below before you go on to the next set of questions.

Further hints

- Did you notice in questions 3 and 8 that I reversed the method? Let's look at question 8 again. Instead of asking you what percentage 23 out of 25 is, I told you that 23 = 92% and asked you to find the number that was equal to 100%. In this case you need to find out how many percent 1 is worth first. Do it like this:

  23 = 92%

  So to find out how many percent 1 is you must divide:

  $92 \div 23 = 4$

  So you now know that 1 = 4%.

  To get to 100% you must multiply 4% by 25 and so you do the same to the 1. So the final total is 25. Watch out for these.

- But what happens when a fraction has a denominator which is not a factor of 100? Often in these cases you can simplify the fraction first to make the denominator a factor of 100 and then multiply up in the usual way. Look at this next example.

Example

Helen has a chocolate bar with 12 pieces. She ate 9 pieces.
What percentage of 12 is this?

Write your fraction and then simplify it like this:

$$\frac{9 \div 3}{12 \div 3} = \frac{3}{4}$$

Now you can see that $^9/_{12}$ is equal to $^3/_4$ and you can turn that into a percentage easily in the usual way.

$$\frac{3 \times 25}{4 \times 25} = \frac{75}{100} = 75\%$$

LESSON 6 PART 2

My Time

My Score

Now let's try some more. Do your workings on a spare piece of paper and then mark your answers on the opposite page. You have 20 minutes to complete this task. Watch out for those fractions you'll need to simplify. Write the time you took and your score in the boxes above once you've finished. Remember to ask an adult to mark these for you.

1 Francis scored 20 out of 40 in a maths test. What was his percentage?

2 If 18 out of 30 students in a class brought their swimming kit to school, what percentage forgot theirs?

3 Faisal calculates that he scored 70% in his science test. If the test was out of 10, how many questions did he get correct?

4 Amy bought a pizza and cut it into 15 slices. She and her friends ate 12 slices – what percentage was this?

5 A school booked 3 coaches, each of which had 50 seats. If 120 of the seats were used, what percentage remained empty?

6 The local council interviewed 200 people. Of these, 150 said they liked clean streets. What percentage is this?

7 In a street of 36 houses, 18 needed a new roof. What percentage of houses did not need a new roof?

8 If Haley scored 75% in a test and got 30 questions correct, what was the test out of?

9 Twelve-sixteenths of students at a school always complete their homework on time. What percentage is this?

10 If 64 out of 80 people from a village catch the train to work, what percentage does not?

LESSON 6 PART 2: ANSWER SHEET

Mark your answer by putting a horizontal line in 1 of the boxes, as in the example below.

Example:

50% ☐
25% ☐
72% ☒
80% ☐
18% ☐

1	2	3	4
20% ☐	18% ☐	5 ☐	12% ☐
40% ☐	30% ☐	6 ☐	15% ☐
60% ☐	40% ☐	7 ☐	27% ☐
50% ☐	60% ☐	8 ☐	60% ☐
75% ☐	12% ☐	9 ☐	80% ☐

5	6	7	8
20% ☐	50% ☐	50% ☐	100 ☐
120% ☐	150% ☐	18% ☐	50 ☐
150% ☐	200% ☐	36% ☐	40 ☐
60% ☐	5% ☐	54% ☐	30 ☐
80% ☐	75% ☐	16% ☐	25 ☐

9	10
75% ☐	64% ☐
12% ☐	80% ☐
16% ☐	144% ☐
28% ☐	16% ☐
88% ☐	20% ☐

LESSON 7 Calculating Probability

In this exercise you'll need to calculate how likely an outcome is; that is, what the probability is that an outcome will occur.

Probability is how likely something is to happen.

To do this, you work out all the possible outcomes and all the favourable outcomes (the likelihood of a favourable outcome is what you need to work out). Then you set these out as a fraction. The number of possible outcomes becomes the denominator and the number of favourable outcomes becomes the numerator. Let's look at an example.

Example

A box contains 12 chocolates, of which 7 are milk chocolates and 5 are dark chocolates. Dawn picks out a chocolate at random. What is the probability that it will be a milk chocolate?

First work out the possible outcomes. There will be 12 of these as there is a total of 12 chocolates in the box. You must include all of them even though you're interested in the milk chocolates only; 12 will be your denominator.

Next, you calculate what the favourable outcomes are. There are 7 of these as you want to know the probability of the milk chocolates. This becomes your numerator. The answer would look like this: $\underline{7/12}$

HELPFUL HINTS

- Probability can be expressed as a percentage as well as fraction.
- Remember how to convert fractions to percentages. Take a look back at lesson 6 if you've forgotten this.
- Your answer should be a fraction in its simplest form. Take a look back at lesson 4 if you've forgotten this.

LESSON 7 PART 1

My Time

My Score

Now look at the questions below. Work them out on some scrap paper and then mark your answers on the grids opposite. You have 20 minutes to complete this task. Write the time you took and your score in the boxes above once you've finished.

A A box contains 2 yellow pencils, 3 green pencils, 6 red pencils, 4 blue pencils and 5 silver pencils. If you pick out a pencil at random, what is the probability that you will pick a:

1 Green pencil?

2 Blue pencil?

3 Yellow pencil?

4 Red pencil?

5 Silver pencil?

B At the summer fair lucky dip, there are 7 sweets, 3 teddy bears, 10 toys, 6 games and 4 face paints as prizes. Picking a prize at random, what is the probability you will pick a:

6 Teddy bear?

7 Toy?

8 Game?

9 Sweet?

10 Face paint?

LESSON 7 PART 1: ANSWER SHEET

Mark your answer by putting a horizontal line in 1 of the boxes, as in the example below.

Example:

$^4/_{12}$ ☐
$^5/_{12}$ ☐
$^6/_{12}$ ☐
$^7/_{12}$ ☒
$^8/_{12}$ ☐

1	2	3	4	5
$^3/_{10}$ ☐	$^4/_{10}$ ☐	$^2/_5$ ☐	$^6/_{10}$ ☐	$^1/_5$ ☐
$^3/_{15}$ ☐	$^4/_{15}$ ☐	$^2/_{10}$ ☐	$^3/_{10}$ ☐	$^1/_4$ ☐
$^3/_{20}$ ☐	$^4/_{17}$ ☐	$^2/_{15}$ ☐	$^6/_{14}$ ☐	$^1/_{20}$ ☐
$^3/_{17}$ ☐	$^4/_{23}$ ☐	$^2/_{17}$ ☐	$^3/_{20}$ ☐	$^1/_{10}$ ☐
$^3/_{23}$ ☐	$^1/_5$ ☐	$^1/_{10}$ ☐	$^6/_{17}$ ☐	$^1/_{15}$ ☐

6	7	8	9	10
$^3/_{27}$ ☐	$^{10}/_{20}$ ☐	20% ☐	$^7/_{30}$ ☐	$^4/_{15}$ ☐
$^3/_{33}$ ☐	$^1/_{30}$ ☐	30% ☐	$^7/_{23}$ ☐	$^2/_{15}$ ☐
$^1/_{10}$ ☐	$^3/_{30}$ ☐	40% ☐	$^7/_{20}$ ☐	$^6/_{15}$ ☐
$^3/_{20}$ ☐	$^1/_3$ ☐	50% ☐	$^7/_{15}$ ☐	$^3/_{15}$ ☐
$^3/_{10}$ ☐	$^{10}/_{15}$ ☐	60% ☐	$^7/_{10}$ ☐	$^5/_{15}$ ☐

How Did You Do? Let's Find Out!

Here are the correct answers. You may mark your answers to these questions yourself.

1 $^3/_{20}$

2 $^1/_5$

3 $^1/_{10}$

4 $^3/_{10}$

5 $^1/_4$

6 $^1/_{10}$

7 $^1/_3$

8 20%

9 $^7/_{30}$

10 $^2/_{15}$

If you scored 8 or more out of 10

This is a good score but if you scored 8 or 9, try to improve in the next part of the lesson. Check where you went wrong and look at the further hints on the next page before you move on to the next set of questions.

If you scored 6 to 7 out of 10

This score isn't too bad, but you need to score higher next time. Check which answers you got wrong and make sure you understand how to work out probability before you move on. Also, check that you didn't make a mistake when marking your answers on the grid. Have a look at the further hints below and then move on to the next set of questions.

If you scored fewer than 6 out of 10

You need to practise probability questions a bit more. Read the following advice before you move on to the next set of questions.

⇨ Do you understand what to do? If not, get an adult to go over the instructions with you again. Then have a look at the questions you got wrong and try to understand why you didn't get the right answer.

⇨ Did you lose your place or put the wrong answer on the answer grid? This is a common mistake so make sure you're careful when you mark your final answer.

Further hints

⇨ Sometimes probability can be expressed in words, such as:
Certain: something that will definitely happen.
Likely: something that has a better than 50% chance of happening.
Even chance: something that has exactly a 50% chance of happening.
Unlikely: something that has a less than 50% chance of happening.
Impossible: something that cannot happen.

⇨ Watch out for questions that use words.

⇨ Watch out for questions that use diagrams. When calculating your answer for a diagram question, you must make sure that each part of the diagram is the same size. Look at the example below.

Example

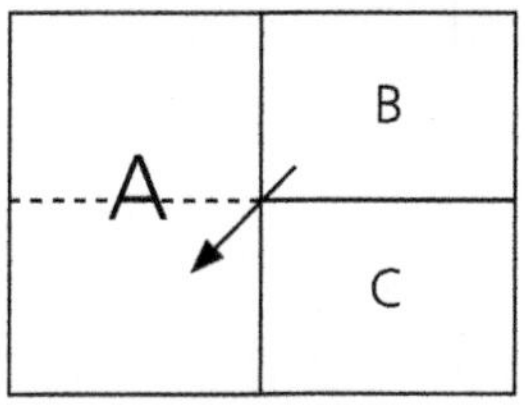

In this game, what is the probability of spinning the letter A?

In this diagram you cannot say there is a 1 in 3 chance of spinning letter A simply because there are 3 letters and boxes. To calculate the problem accurately all the areas must be of equal size so you add a line (the dotted line) through A's box. Now you can see that there are 4 equally sized boxes for the spinner to land in. A has 2 of these and so has a 2 out of 4 chance of the spinner landing on it, which is equal to 50%.

LESSON 7 PART 2

My Time | **My Score**

Let's have a go at some more. Do your workings on some scrap paper and then mark your answers on the corresponding grids opposite. You have 20 minutes to complete this task. Write the time you took and your score in the boxes above once you've finished. Remember to get an adult to mark these for you.

A A sweet shop jar contains 5 butterscotch sweets, 3 toffees, 4 lemon drops, 8 fizzy tops, 13 liquorice squares and 7 chewy sweets. If you put your hand in the jar and picked a sweet at random, what would be the probability of picking a:

1 Fizzy top?

2 Toffee?

3 Lemon drop?

4 Butterscotch?

5 Chewy sweet?

6 Liquorice square?

B At the summer fair a game is played by spinning an arrow. What is the probability of the arrow landing on:

7 An odd number?

8 A 4?

9 A 5?

10 A number smaller than 4?

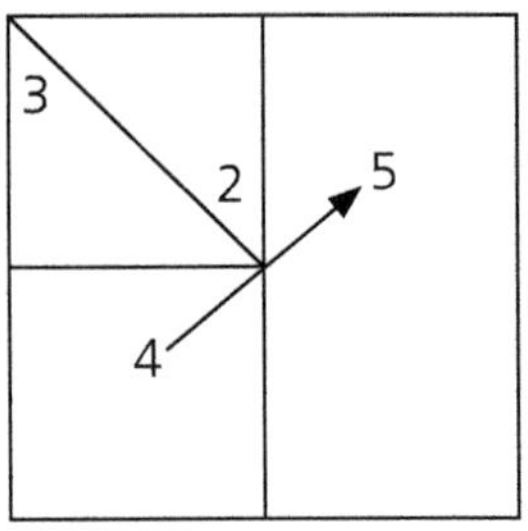

LESSON 7 PART 2: ANSWER SHEET

Mark your answer by putting a horizontal line in 1 of the boxes, as in the example below.

Example:

4/12 ☐
5/12 ☐
6/12 ☐
7/12 ⊟
8/12 ☐

1	2	3	4	5
1/2 ☐	3/37 ☐	1/4 ☐	1/5 ☐	7/33 ☐
1/3 ☐	3/43 ☐	1/5 ☐	1/6 ☐	7/40 ☐
1/4 ☐	3/40 ☐	1/6 ☐	1/7 ☐	7/47 ☐
1/5 ☐	3/30 ☐	1/8 ☐	1/8 ☐	1/7 ☐
1/6 ☐	3/33 ☐	1/10 ☐	1/9 ☐	1/9 ☐

6	7	8	9	10
13/40 ☐	3/8 ☐	1/2 ☐	1/2 ☐	1/2 ☐
13/53 ☐	1/2 ☐	1/3 ☐	1/3 ☐	1/3 ☐
13/27 ☐	1/3 ☐	1/4 ☐	1/4 ☐	1/4 ☐
1/4 ☐	1/4 ☐	1/5 ☐	1/5 ☐	1/5 ☐
1/5 ☐	5/8 ☐	1/6 ☐	1/6 ☐	1/6 ☐

LESSON 8 Calculating Ratios

A ratio is a way of comparing the amount of one thing with another or what you use to compare parts of a whole.

For example, I add in two spoons of sugar for each cup of coffee I have. The ratio of spoons of sugar to cups of coffee is 2:1.

In this exercise you'll need to use a ratio to help you calculate your answers. There are several types of ratio question and I've outlined them for you here. Let's look at some examples.

Example 1

In a class of 30 children, 17 are girls. Write the ratio of girls to boys.

For the question above, you must remember two points. Firstly, the total number of children is 30 so if there are 17 girls, there must be 13 boys. Secondly, make sure you write the ratio in the correct order. The question asks for the ratio of girls to boys so you should write the number of girls first. So your answer should look like this: 17:13

Example 2

The ratio of windows to doors of a house is 4:1.
If there are 20 windows, how many doors are there?

In this example, you're given the ratio and have to use it to calculate the answer. If you're told that the ratio for windows is 4:1 and the number of actual windows is 20, then the ratio must have been multiplied by 5. You must do the same to the other part of the ratio.

So the number of doors is: $1 \times 5 = 5$

LESSON 8 PART 1

My Time

My Score

Have a look at the questions below. Work them out on a separate sheet of paper and then mark your answers on the opposite page. You have 20 minutes to complete this task. Write the time you took and your score in the boxes above once you've finished.

1. If the ratio of sugar lumps to cups of coffee is 3:1, how many lumps of sugar are needed for 6 cups of coffee?
2. Karl is watching the traffic go along his street. He notices that for every 2 motorbikes, there are 5 cars. If 50 cars go along his street in 1 day, how many motorbikes also pass that way in the same time?
3. An office employs 23 members of staff and 7 are managers. What is the ratio of workers to managers?
4. A supermarket sells 350 jars of tea and coffee. If 129 of the jars are coffee, what is the ratio of tea to coffee sold?
5. A student calculates that for every fiction book he reads, he also reads 3 non-fiction books. He read 27 non-fiction books in a term; how many fiction books did he also read?
6. A teacher has 4 pencils for every 3 rulers in her class. If there are 28 pencils, how many rulers are there?
7. Annabel makes a fruit smoothie by using a ratio of 3 bananas to 7 strawberries. If she makes 5 of these smoothies for her friends, how many strawberries will she need?
8. A store cupboard contains 40 tins of food. There are 33 tins of tuna and the rest are sardines. What is the ratio of tuna to sardines?
9. To make maroon paint a ratio of 5 red to 3 blue tins is used. How many tins of blue are needed if 40 tins of red are used?
10. In a box of 26 pens, 7 are red and the rest are blue. What is the ratio of blue to red pens?

LESSON 8 PART 1: ANSWER SHEET

Mark your answer by putting a horizontal line in 1 of the boxes, as in the examples below.

Example 1:

17:30 ▭
30:13 ▭
30:17 ▭
17:13 ▬
13:17 ▭

Example 2:

1 ▭
2 ▭
3 ▭
4 ▭
5 ▬

1	2	3	4
9 ▭	100 ▭	7:23 ▭	350:129 ▭
4 ▭	48 ▭	23:7 ▭	221:129 ▭
18 ▭	20 ▭	16:7 ▭	221:350 ▭
10 ▭	40 ▭	7:16 ▭	350:221 ▭
7 ▭	45 ▭	16:23 ▭	350:221 ▭

5	6	7	8
30 ▭	32 ▭	10 ▭	33:40 ▭
24 ▭	31 ▭	12 ▭	40:33 ▭
9 ▭	7 ▭	15 ▭	7:40 ▭
12 ▭	21 ▭	35 ▭	7:33 ▭
18 ▭	24 ▭	40 ▭	33:7 ▭

9	10
43 ▭	7:19 ▭
45 ▭	19:7 ▭
37 ▭	19:26 ▭
35 ▭	26:19 ▭
24 ▭	26:7 ▭

How Did You Do? Let's Find Out!

Here are the correct answers. You may mark your answers to these questions yourself.

1 18

2 20

3 16:7

4 221:129

5 9

6 21

7 35

8 33:7

9 24

10 19:7

If you scored 8 or more out of 10

This is a good score but if you scored 8 or 9, try to improve in the next part of the lesson. Check where you went wrong and look at the further hint on the next page before you move on to the next set of questions.

If you scored 6 to 7 out of 10

Not bad, but to help you score higher next time, check which answers you got wrong and make sure you understand the difference between the two types of question before you move on. Check also that you didn't make a mistake when marking your answers on the sheet. Have a look at the further hint on the next page and then move on to the next set of questions.

If you scored fewer than 6 out of 10

Scoring fewer than 6 means you'll need to improve. Read the advice below to help you before you move on to the next set of questions.

➪ Do you understand what to do? If not, ask an adult to go over the instructions with you again. Then have a look at the questions you got wrong and try to understand why. Make sure you do this thoroughly, as it will only get more difficult if you don't understand.

➪ Read the further hint below before you move on and make sure you understand all of the different types of questions.

Further hint

Watch out for the following type of question which requires several steps to calculate the correct answer.

Example

Three boys, Marvin, Harold and Malik, collect football stickers. For every sticker Marvin collects, Harold collects 2 and Malik collects 5. If the boys have collected 64 stickers between them, how many does Malik have?

The steps to solve this question are:

1 Work out the ratio for each boy. The question says for every sticker Marvin collects – so Marvin collects 1 each time, Harold 2 and Malik 5. Set them out like this:

Marvin: 1
Harold: 2
Malik: 5

2 Add these together. 1 + 2 + 5 = 8.

3 Take this answer and use it to divide the total number of stickers the boys have between them:

64 ÷ 8 = 8.

4 Multiply this answer by each boy's original ratio and you'll know how many stickers each boy has:

Marvin: 1 × 8 = 8
Harold: 2 × 8 = 16
Malik: 5 × 8 = 40

And if you add all these up, they make 64 – that's a good way to check your answer. So Malik has 40 stickers.

LESSON 8 PART 2

My Time

My Score

Let's practise a few more. Work the questions out on a separate sheet of paper and then mark your answers on the corresponding grids. You have 20 minutes to complete this task. Watch out for the style of question I showed you in the further hint. Write the time you took and your score in the boxes above once you've finished. Remember to get an adult to mark these for you.

1 A factory makes a ratio of 7 yellow to 4 blue plates. If it made 350 yellow plates in a day, how many blue plates did it make?

2 A class at school is made up of a ratio of 5 girls to 3 boys. If there are 32 children in the class, how many are girls?

3 33 people work in an office. If 17 are female what is the female to male ratio?

4 Ben and Madge raised £45 for a local charity. For every £3 Ben raised, Madge raised £6. How much money did Ben raise?

5 A store sells a ratio of clothes to toys of 6:5. If 60 clothes were sold, how many toys were also sold?

6 In an aquarium there are 37 fish: 17 are clown fish and the rest are goldfish. What is the ratio of goldfish to clown fish?

7 A shop sells tins of dog and cat food. Each day 43 tins are sold, of which 19 are cat food. What is the ratio of dog to cat food that is sold?

8 A teacher has 3 calculators to every maths book in her class. If she has 42 calculators, how many maths books does she have?

9 If a bus has a ratio of 4 adults to every child and there are 35 people on the bus, how many children are there?

10 A student revises each week for her exams. For every hour she studies geography she spends 2 hours on maths. She studies geography 1 hour each week. For how many hours has she studied maths after 7 weeks?

LESSON 8 PART 2: ANSWER SHEET

Mark your answer by putting a horizontal line in 1 of the boxes, as in the examples below.

Example 1:

17:30
30:13
30:17
17:13 (marked)
13:17

Example 2:

1
2
3
4
5 (marked)

1
322
28
50
200
150

2
15
8
20
27
29

3
17:33
17:16
16:23
16:17
33:16

4
£15
£18
£27
£39
£36

5
11
49
30
50
20

6
37:17
20:17
20:37
37:20
17:37

7
43:19
19:43
19:24
24:19
24:43

8
39
14
28
31
15

9
30
7
28
14
21

10
7
14
21
28
35

LESSON 9 Calculating Proportion

Proportion is the comparative relationship between two objects.

Often, this is used in questions about costs. For example 1 pencil might cost 12p, so 2 would cost 24p. The cost is directly linked to the number of pencils and the proportion does not change no matter the amount of pencils.

In this exercise you're given two pieces of information which relate to each other. You'll be asked to apply that knowledge to work out a problem. Let's have a look at some examples.

Example 1

If 7 shirts in a shop cost £63 in total, find the cost of 5 shirts.

First you need to find out the cost of 1 shirt. You do this by dividing £63 by 7.

£63 ÷ 7 = £9

So now you know that 1 shirt costs £9.

To find the cost of 5 shirts, you simply multiply the £9 by 5.

£9 × 5 = 45.

Therefore the final answer would be £45.

Example 2

How much does 100g of salt cost when 500g costs 85p?

This question is a little trickier since you're dealing in hundreds of grams. A good way is to draw a simple table with the information set out in order, like this:

÷ 5

500g	85p
100g	?

Look at the proportional relationship between 500g and 100g. To get from 500g to 100g you must divide by 5. Therefore, you must also divide 85p by 5 to find the correct cost of 100g of salt.

85p ÷ 5 = 17p

So your answer would be 17p.

LESSON 9 PART 1

My Time

My Score

Work through the questions below. Do your workings on some scrap paper and then mark your answers on the next page. You have 20 minutes to complete this task. Write the time you took and your score in the boxes above once you've finished.

1. If 8 sweets cost 72p in total, how much would 11 sweets cost?
2. A lift carries 6 children with a total weight of 240kg. How much weight would the lift carry if it was carrying 4 children?
3. If 10 calculators cost £13, how much would 1 cost?
4. If 12 chairs cost £132, how much would 7 chairs cost?
5. A 150cm length of silk costs £2.70. How much would a 50cm length of silk cost?
6. How much would 40ml of drink cost at £1.12 per 280ml?
7. How far would a car travel in an hour if it moved 20km in 15 minutes?
8. If 6 cartons of milk hold 18 litres, how many litres do 15 cartons hold?
9. A shop is selling umbrellas at £32 for 8. How much would 3 umbrellas cost?
10. If a dog walks 3km in 10 minutes what speed is it travelling at in km/hour?

LESSON 9 PART 1: ANSWER SHEET

Mark your answer by putting a horizontal line in 1 of the boxes, as in the examples below.

Example 1:

£63 ▭
£9 ▭
£54 ▭
£45 ▬
£36 ▭

Example 2:

85p ▭
17p ▬
34p ▭
51p ▭
68p ▭

1

8p ▭
20p ▭
96p ▭
99p ▭
83p ▭

2

234kg ▭
40kg ▭
60kg ▭
160kg ▭
80kg ▭

3

£0.13 ▭
£1.30 ▭
£13.00 ▭
£1.03 ▭
£0.03 ▭

4

£19 ▭
£7 ▭
£12 ▭
£77 ▭
£84 ▭

5

£1.35 ▭
£0.90 ▭
£2.20 ▭
£1.20 ▭
£0.70 ▭

6

28p ▭
16p ▭
40p ▭
24p ▭
£1.60 ▭

7

35km ▭
80km ▭
15km ▭
40km ▭
60km ▭

8

39 litres ▭
108 litres ▭
90 litres ▭
45 litres ▭
24 litres ▭

9

£35 ▭
£24 ▭
£4 ▭
£11 ▭
£12 ▭

10

60km/h ▭
18km/h ▭
30km/h ▭
45km/h ▭
15km/h ▭

How Did You Do? Let's Find Out!

Here are the correct answers. You may mark your answers to these questions yourself.

1. 99p
2. 160kg
3. £1.30
4. £77
5. £0.90
6. 16p
7. 80km
8. 45 litres
9. £12
10. 18km/h

If you scored 8 or more out of 10

How did you find the proportion questions? They can be quite tricky so be cautious, read the question carefully, don't rush and you should be fine. This is a good score but if you scored 8 or 9, use the next part of the lesson to improve your score. Look at the further hint on the next page before you move on to the next set of questions.

If you scored 6 to 7 out of 10

Not a bad score, but check where you went wrong to help you to score higher next time. Check which answers you got wrong and make sure you understand the difference between the types of question before you move on.

Also, check that you didn't make a mistake when marking your answers on the answer grid. Read the further hint below and then move on to the next set of questions.

If you scored fewer than 6 out of 10

You'll need to do some more practice questions to improve your score. Read the following advice to help you improve before you move on to the next set of questions.

- Do you understand what to do? If not, get an adult to go over the instructions with you again. Then have a look at any questions you got wrong and try to understand why your answers are incorrect.

- Read the further hint below before you move on to the next set of questions.

Further hint

Watch out for questions that mix units of measurement. A question might ask you to find the price of 50cm when you've been given the price of 1.5m. In this case you must make the link between centimetres and metres. Since there are 100cm in a metre you know that 1.5m is the same as 150cm. The question then becomes much easier. This can be done with all types of metric measurement (see page 124 for a list of these).

LESSON 9 PART 2

My Time

My Score

Now have a go at these questions. Work them out on some scrap paper and then mark your answers on the answer sheet. You have 20 minutes to complete this task. Write the time you took and your score in the boxes above once you've finished. And remember to get an adult to mark these for you.

1. If 12 sweets cost £1.44 in total, how much money would 7 sweets cost?
2. 7 cars weigh 63 tonnes; how much do 5 weigh?
3. If a car travels 19km in 12 minutes, how far will it travel in 1 hour?
4. If half a kilogram of peanuts costs £1.15, how much do 200g cost?
5. 3.5m of silk costs £4.90. How much would 50cm of silk cost?
6. If 2 litres of petrol costs £2.24, how much will 500ml cost?
7. If 8 football shirts cost £160, how much do 5 cost?
8. If 4 egg boxes contain 52 eggs, how many eggs will 3 boxes hold?
9. If 7 lemons weigh 84g, what would 15 lemons weigh?
10. What is the cost of 1.1kg of apples at 50p per 500g?

LESSON 9 PART 2: ANSWER SHEET

Mark your answer by putting a horizontal line in 1 of the boxes, as in the examples below.

Example 1:

£63
£9
£54
£45 [marked]
£36

Example 2:

85p
17p [marked]
34p
51p
68p

1

£1.56
£1.32
£0.84
£0.20
£0.60

2

58 tonnes
56 tonnes
35 tonnes
45 tonnes
28 tonnes

3

31km
60km
95km
41km
48km

4

23p
46p
22p
62p
200p

5

50p
35p
70p
120p
98p

6

£1.12
£2.76
£2.50
£0.24
£0.56

7

£20
£168
£152
£40
£100

8

208
13
39
156
12

9

12g
99g
91g
180g
105g

10

£1.10
£5.50
£1.60
£0.25
£0.10

LESSON 10 Calculating Areas and Perimeters

Perimeter is the distance around the outside of a shape. It's calculated by adding up all the sides of the shape.

Area tells us how much surface a shape has. It's calculated by multiplying the length by the width (or breadth) for regular squares and rectangles.

In this exercise you'll need know the difference between area and perimeter and also how to calculate both of them. Let's look at some examples.

Example 1

Calculate the perimeter of the shape below:

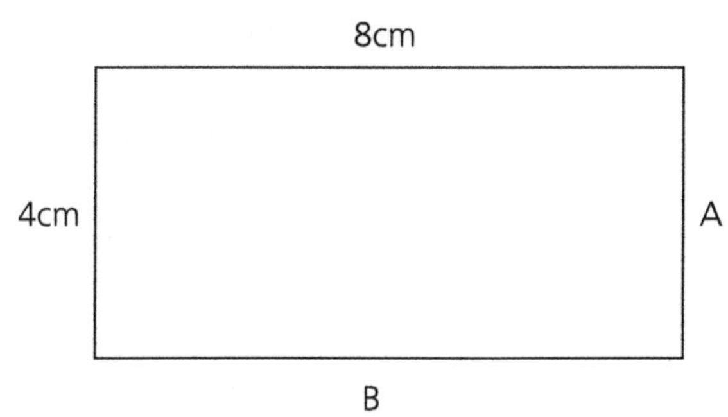

To find the perimeter you must add all the sides of the shape; not just those with measurements. Where there are no measurements you must work them out and then add them. You can work out that side A is 4cm as it's opposite a side measuring 4cm. You know the sides are the same since the shape is a rectangle so opposite sides are equal in length. In the same way you know that side B is equal to 8cm.

You should now add these up: 8 + 8 + 4 + 4 = 24

So the answer is <u>24cm</u>.

Example 2

Calculate the area of the shape above.

In this case you do not need to know every side, just the length and the width of the shape. So you would multiply these.

$8 \times 4 = 32$

The answer is <u>32cm²</u>

Notice how you would also write a '2' to show that the answer is in square cm.

LESSON 10 PART 1

My Time

My Score

Next, try the questions below. Do your workings on a spare piece of paper and then mark your answers on the opposite page. You have 20 minutes to complete this task. Write the time you took and your score in the boxes above once you've finished.

1. If a rectangle is 9cm long and 5cm wide, what is its perimeter?
2. If a field is 80m long and 30m wide, what is its area?
3. What is the numerical difference between the area and the perimeter of a rectangle with length 11cm and width 7cm?
4. One side of a square measures 8mm. What is its perimeter?
5. A rectangle has a perimeter of 14cm. If it is 5cm long, how wide is it?
6. The side of a square is 12m long. What is its area?
7. If the area of a rectangle is $42m^2$ and it is 6m wide, what is its length?
8. If the perimeter of a room is 52m, what could its length and width be?
9. If the area of a sports ground is $80m^2$, what could its length and width be?
10. What is the area of the shape below?

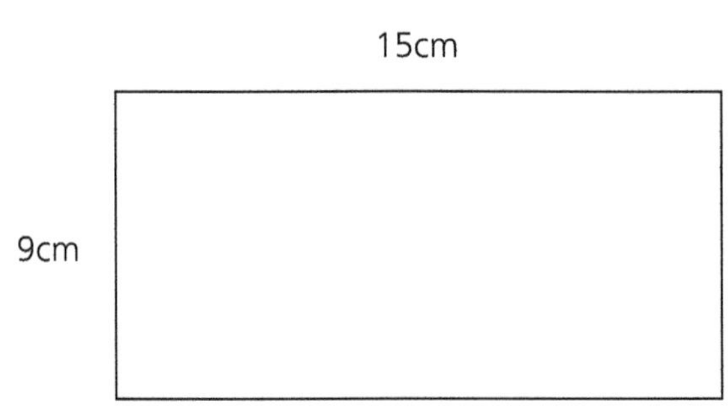

LESSON 10 PART 1: ANSWER SHEET

Mark your answer by putting a horizontal line in 1 of the boxes, as in the examples below.

Example 1:

- 8cm
- 4cm
- 12cm
- 24cm (marked)
- 32cm

Example 2:

- $12cm^2$
- $32cm^2$ (marked)
- $36cm^2$
- $40cm^2$
- $44cm^2$

1

- 14cm
- 19cm
- 23cm
- 28cm
- 32cm

2

- $110m^2$
- $240m^2$
- $2,400m^2$
- $24,000m^2$
- $1,100m^2$

3

- 77cm
- 41cm
- 36cm
- 22cm
- 18cm

4

- 8mm
- 16mm
- 24mm
- 32mm
- 40mm

5

- 7cm
- 5cm
- 4cm
- 3cm
- 2cm

6

- $24m^2$
- $48m^2$
- $120m^2$
- $132m^2$
- $144m^2$

7

- 36m
- 7m
- 6m
- 5m
- 4m

8

- 10m, 5m
- 9m, 4m
- 20m, 6m
- 15m, 2m
- 25m, 2m

9

- 11m, 9m
- 10m, 8m
- 9m, 7m
- 12m, 6m
- 8m, 7m

10

- $24cm^2$
- $95cm^2$
- $90cm^2$
- $105cm^2$
- $135cm^2$

How Did You Do? Let's Find Out!

Here are the correct answers. You may mark your answers to these questions yourself.

1. 28cm
2. 2,400m^2
3. 41cm
4. 32mm
5. 2cm
6. 144m^2
7. 7m
8. 20m, 6m
9. 10m, 8m
10. 135cm^2

If you scored 8 or more out of 10

This is a good score but if you scored 8 or 9, try to improve in the next part of the lesson. Check where you went wrong and look at the further hints on the next page before you move on to the next set of questions.

If you scored 6 to 7 out of 10

Not too bad but try to score higher next time by checking the answers you got wrong and making sure you understand the difference between area and perimeter before you move on. Check that you didn't make a mistake when marking the answer sheet. Read the further hints below and then move on to the next set of questions.

If you scored fewer than 6 out of 10

You really need to improve your score so tackle some more practice questions. You should also read the following advice before you move on to the next set of questions.

➪ Do you understand what to do? If not, get an adult to go over the instructions with you again. Then have a look at any questions you got wrong and try to understand why. Make sure you do this thoroughly as it will only get more difficult if you don't understand.

➪ Read the further hints below before you move on.

Further hints

➪ As you probably noticed, there are quite a few ways of asking questions about perimeter and area. Watch out for the questions that require you to work backwards. In question 5, for example, I told you the perimeter was 14cm and the length was 5cm. Since you know you are dealing with a rectangle, you also know there will be 2 different lengths of sides and you must count each twice. So there will be 2 sides of 5cm which makes 10cm in total. You know the final perimeter is 14cm so that leaves 4cm. But this is not the answer since you need 2 sides to make 4cm. So your final answer should be 2cm.

➪ I did the same with question 7, only this time it was with area. I told you the final area was $42m^2$ and that 1 side was 6m. Because you always multiply to find the area, here you do the opposite and so you divide. So $42 \div 6 = 7$m.

➪ I also gave you some tough questions where I told you the area or perimeter and then asked you to work out the length of the sides that would make those amounts. These were questions 8 and 9. In these cases you need to work through the possible answers on the answer grid until you find a pair that works.

LESSON 10 PART 2

My Time | **My Score**

Now let's try these. It's best to work the answers out on some scrap paper and then mark your answers on the opposite page. You have 20 minutes to complete this task. Write the time you took and your score in the boxes above once you've finished. Remember to get an adult to mark these for you.

1 Bill is walking around the outside of his garden, which is 9m long and 3m wide. How far did he walk?

2 The children offer to paint a wall at school. If it measures 4m by 10m and a paint tin will cover $8m^2$, how many tins of paint will they need?

3 What is the difference between the area and perimeter of a square that is 9cm long?

4 Mr Smith measures his kitchen floor. It is 7m long and 2m wide. What is its area?

5 A rectangle has a perimeter of 28cm. If it is 9cm long, how wide is it?

6 The side of a square is 19m. What is its area?

7 If the area of a rectangle is $630m^2$ and it is 90m long, what is its width?

8 If the perimeter of a room is 74m, what could its length and width be?

9 If the area of a sports ground is $280m^2$, what could its length and width be?

10 If shape A is a garden lawn and shape B is a pond, what is the area of the lawn?

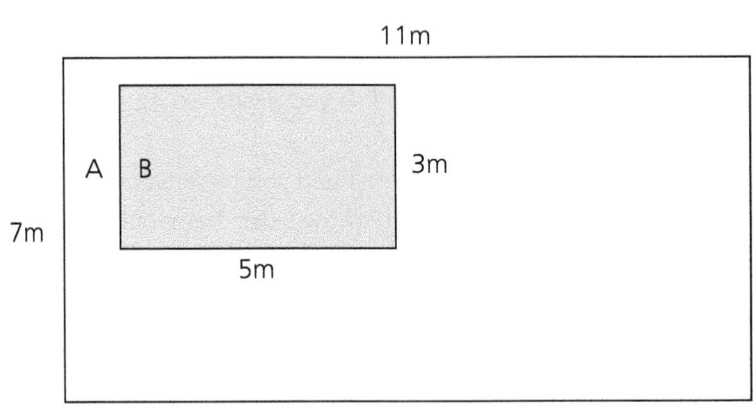

LESSON 10 PART 2: ANSWER SHEET

Mark your answer by putting a horizontal line in 1 of the boxes, as in the examples below.

Example 1:

- 8cm
- 4cm
- 12cm
- 24cm (marked)
- 32cm

Example 2:

- $12cm^2$
- $32cm^2$ (marked)
- $36cm^2$
- $40cm^2$
- $44cm^2$

1

- 12m
- 15m
- 21m
- 26m
- 24m

2

- 1
- 2
- 3
- 4
- 5

3

- 18cm
- 36cm
- 45cm
- 81cm
- 117cm

4

- $9m^2$
- $14m^2$
- $23m^2$
- $18m^2$
- $16m^2$

5

- 19cm
- 18cm
- 10cm
- 5cm
- 3cm

6

- $91m^2$
- $19m^2$
- $361m^2$
- $38m^2$
- $76m^2$

7

- 7m
- 70m
- 54m
- 72m
- 5m

8

- 8m, 4m
- 8m, 10m
- 30m, 14m
- 30m, 7m
- 40m, 4m

9

- 2m, 80m
- 14m, 10m
- 28m, 11m
- 14m, 20m
- 28m, 5m

10

- $92m^2$
- $77m^2$
- $15m^2$
- $62m^2$
- $26m^2$

LESSON 11 Calculating the Area of Right-Angled Triangles and Irregular Shapes

In this exercise you'll need to find the area of a right-angled triangle and the area of irregular shapes – which is slightly different from finding the area of a square or rectangle. To work out the area of a right-angled triangle you'll need to know the length of its base and halve it. Then you'll multiply this number by its height.

A right-angled triangle is one where the angle between the lines of its base and height is 90°. This is often indicated by a box shape in its corner, like the one in example 1 below.

Example 1

What is the area of the triangle shown below?

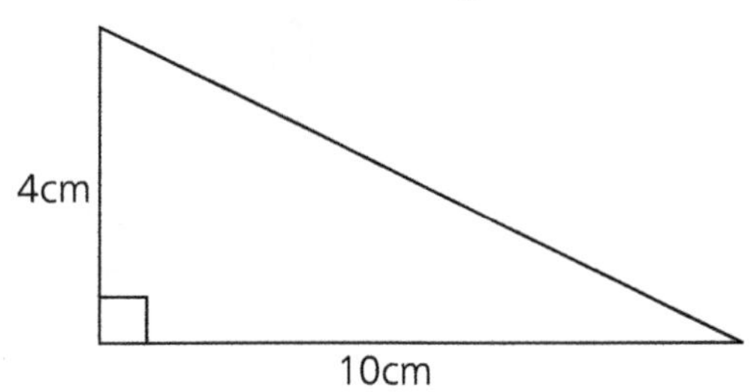

The base of this triangle is 10cm. Half of this is 5cm. Multiply this answer by the height which is 4cm.

So the area = 10 ÷ 2 = 5; 5 × 4 = $\underline{20\text{cm}^2}$

Remember from lesson 10 that you calculate the area of a rectangle or square by multiplying the length by the width (L × W). If a shape is irregular (so it's not rectangular or square), try to divide it into several regular rectangles or squares. Find the area of each of these and add the totals together. See example 2 below.

Example 2

What is the area of the 'L' shape given below?

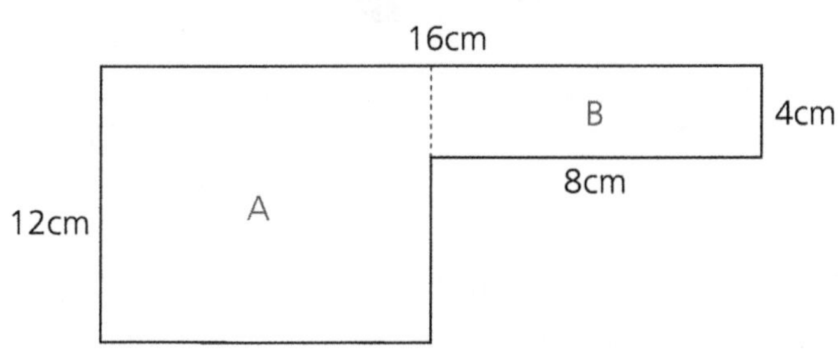

The 'L' shape can be divided into two rectangles shape A and shape B. You can calculate the areas of both of these shapes and then add the totals together.
The area of shape A = 12cm × 8cm = 96cm^2
The area of shape B = 8cm × 4cm = 32cm^2
Therefore the total area = 96cm^2 + 32cm^2 = $\underline{128\text{cm}^2}$

LESSON 11 PART 1

My Time

My Score

Now look at the questions below. Work out the areas on some scrap paper and then mark your answers on the corresponding grids. You have 20 minutes to complete this task. Write the time you took and your score in the boxes above once you've finished.

Find the area of the following shapes:

1

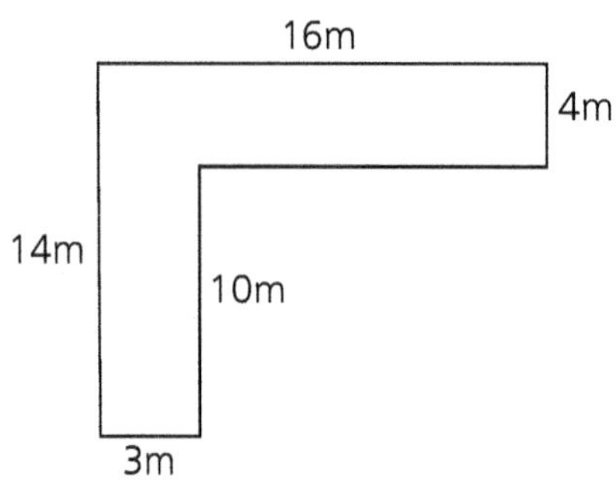

2

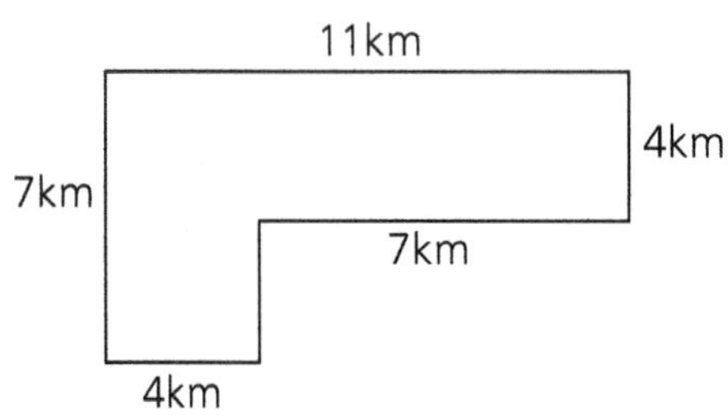

3

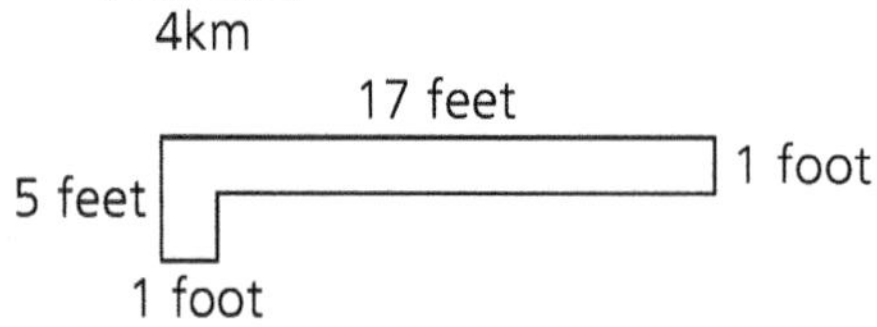

4

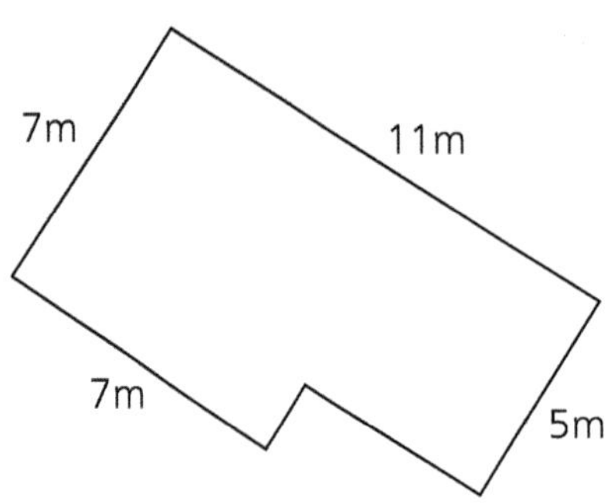

5

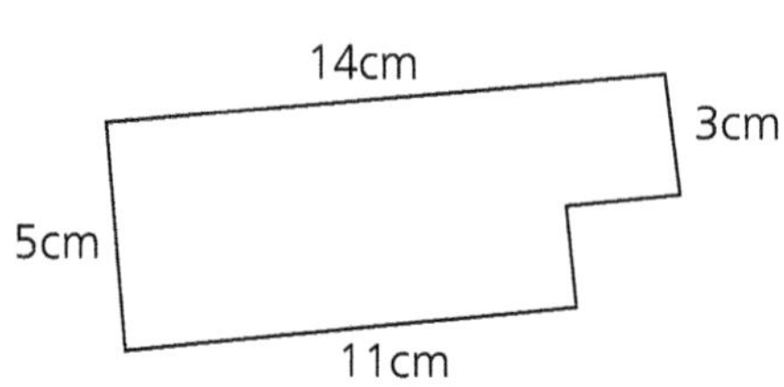

6

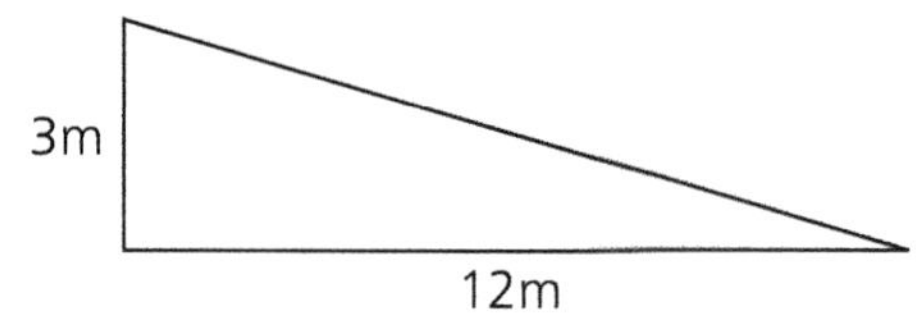

7

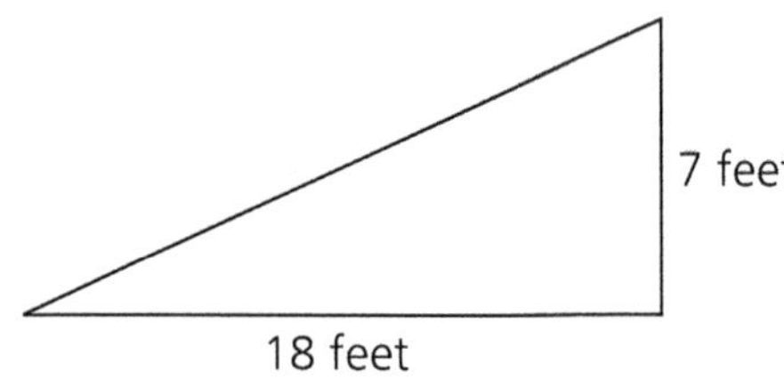

8

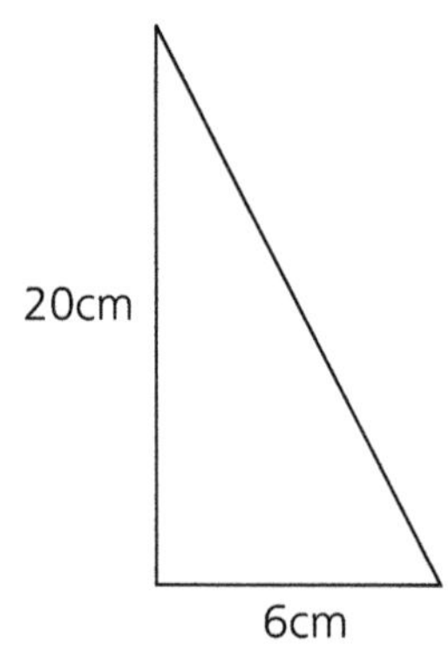

9

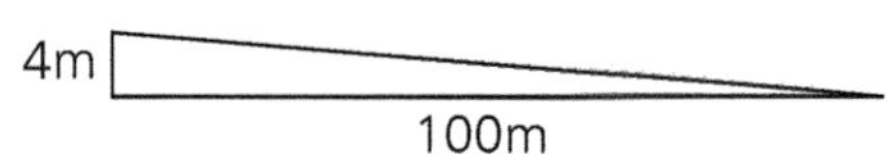

10

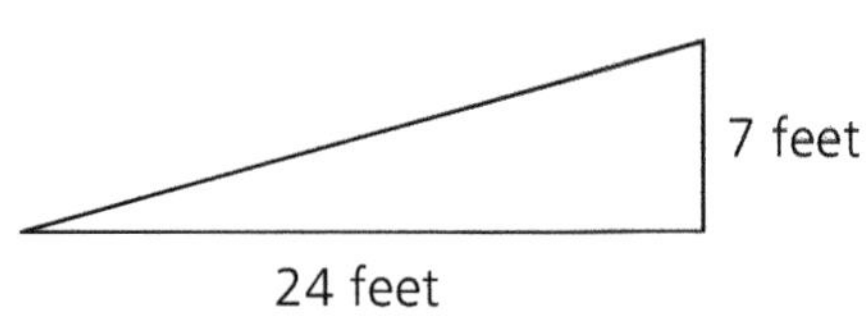

LESSON 11 PART 1: ANSWER SHEET

Mark your answer by putting a horizontal line in 1 of the boxes, as in the examples below.

Example 1:

10cm² ▭
40cm² ▭
14cm² ▭
20cm² ▬
6cm² ▭

Example 2:

64cm² ▭
128cm² ▬
96cm² ▭
192cm² ▭
32cm² ▭

1	2	3	4
224m² ▭	77km² ▭	17ft² ▭	77m² ▭
64m² ▭	28km² ▭	24ft² ▭	49m² ▭
112m² ▭	56km² ▭	21ft² ▭	14m² ▭
42m² ▭	44km² ▭	22ft² ▭	27m² ▭
94m² ▭	121km² ▭	23ft² ▭	69m² ▭

5	6	7	8
22cm² ▭	12m² ▭	7ft² ▭	20cm² ▭
35cm² ▭	36m² ▭	18ft² ▭	26cm² ▭
90cm² ▭	15m² ▭	63ft² ▭	120cm² ▭
99cm² ▭	18m² ▭	126ft² ▭	60cm² ▭
64cm² ▭	9m² ▭	11ft² ▭	30cm² ▭

9	10
400m² ▭	31ft² ▭
300m² ▭	168ft² ▭
200m² ▭	140ft² ▭
100m² ▭	84ft² ▭
50m² ▭	75ft² ▭

How Did You Do? Let's Find Out!

Here are the correct answers. You may mark your answers to these questions yourself.

1. $94m^2$
2. $56km^2$
3. $21ft^2$
4. $69m^2$
5. $64cm^2$
6. $18m^2$
7. $63ft^2$
8. $60cm^2$
9. $200m^2$
10. $84ft^2$

If you scored 8 or more out of 10

This is a good score but if you scored 8 or 9, try and get it up to a 10 in the next part of the lesson. Have a look at where you went wrong to help you do this and look at the further hints on the next page before you move on to the next set of questions.

If you scored 6 to 7 out of 10

Not too bad but to improve your score check the answers you got wrong, and make sure you understand the difference between area and perimeter before you move on. Also, check that you didn't make a mistake when marking your answers on the answer grid. Have a look at the further hints on the next page to help with the next questions.

If you scored fewer than 6 out of 10

Read the following advice and the further hints below to help you improve before you move on to the next set of questions.

➪ Do you understand what to do? If not, get an adult to go over the instructions with you again. Then have a look at any questions you got wrong and try to understand why. Make sure you do this thoroughly, as it will only get more difficult if you don't understand.

➪ Check you thoroughly understand the differences between area and perimeter.

Further hints

➪ As you probably noticed with the 'L' shapes, not all the measurements are given. Be careful as these shapes are sometimes used in perimeter questions and for those you need to find the length of every side before adding them up. Look at the example below.

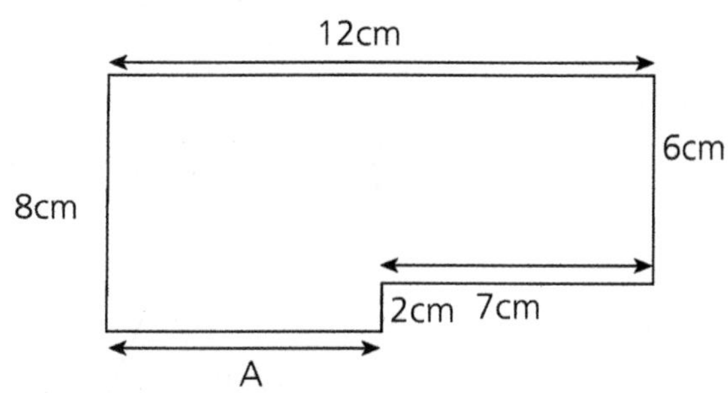

To find the length of side A, compare the other sides which go in the same direction – I've marked them for you with arrows like this: ⟷

By comparing them you can see that the lengths of the 2 shorter sides have to equal the length of the longest side. You know that the longest side is 12cm and 1 of the shorter sides is 7cm so it's just like finding the difference: 12cm – 7cm = 5cm. Side A is 5cm. So the perimeter of this shape is 40cm.

➪ There is another way to find the area of a triangle too. If you note that the base is an odd number and therefore awkward to halve and multiply, check the value of the height. You could halve this instead if you want – it makes no difference to the answer – but remember to only halve one of them and not both!

➪ What happens with triangles when both numbers are odd? In this case simply multiply them then halve the final answer – this is an easier way to work it out.

LESSON 11 PART 2

My Time

My Score

Now let's try some more. Work the questions out on some scrap paper and then mark your answers on the corresponding grids. You have 20 minutes to complete this task. Write the time you took and your score in the boxes above once you've finished. Remember to get an adult to mark these for you.

1 Find the perimeter of this shape.

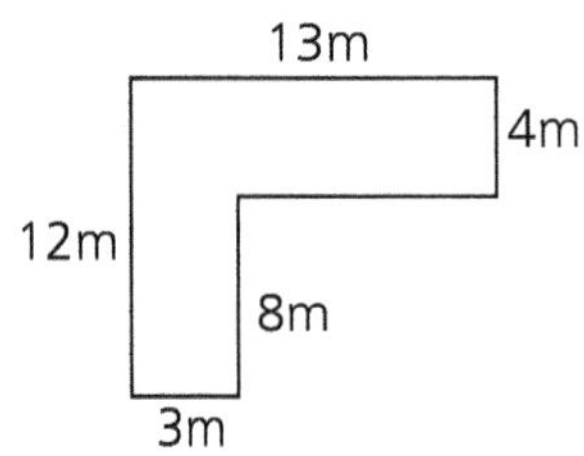

2 Find the area of this shape.

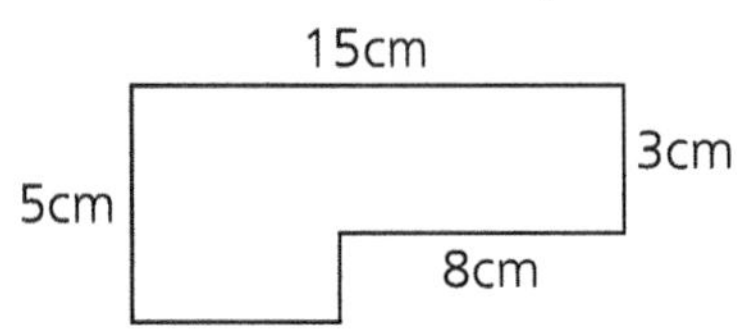

3 Find the perimeter of this shape.

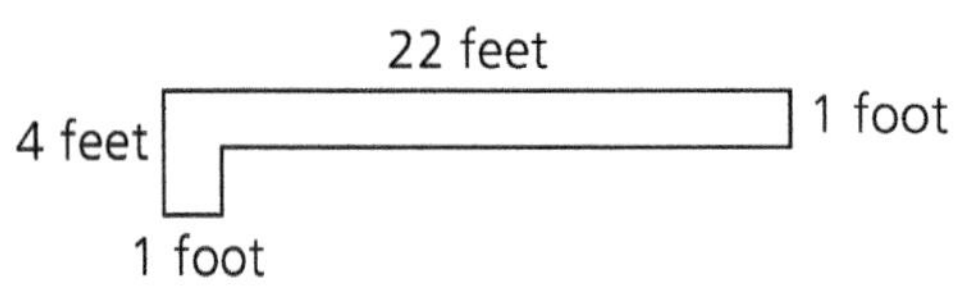

4 Find the area of this shape.

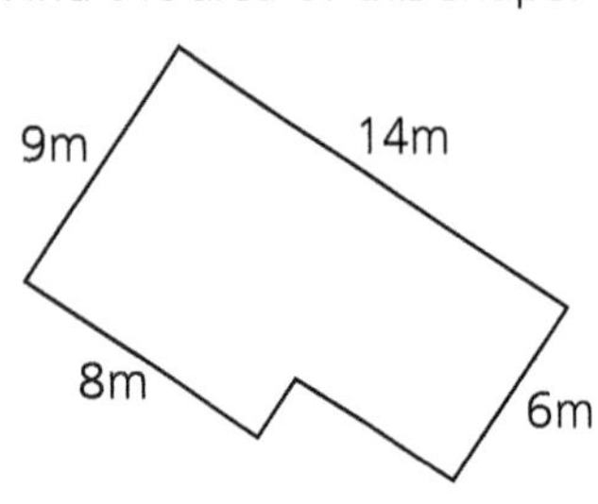

5 Find the perimeter of this shape.

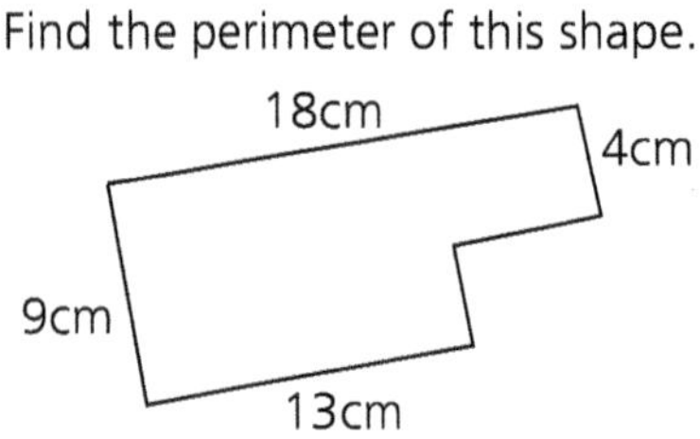

6 Find the area of this shape.

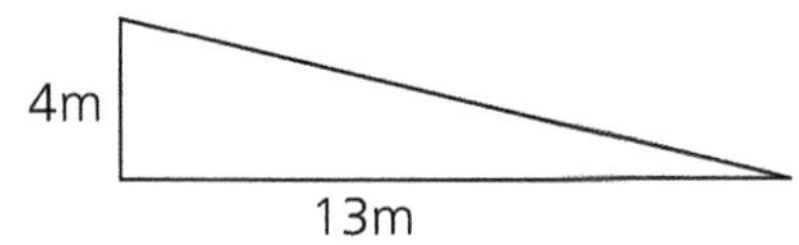

7 Find the area of this shape.

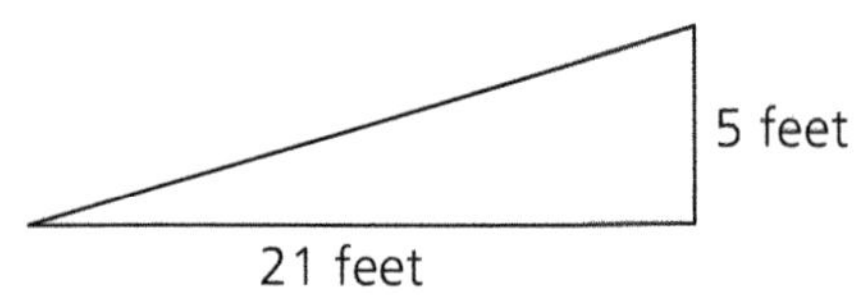

8 Find the area of this shape.

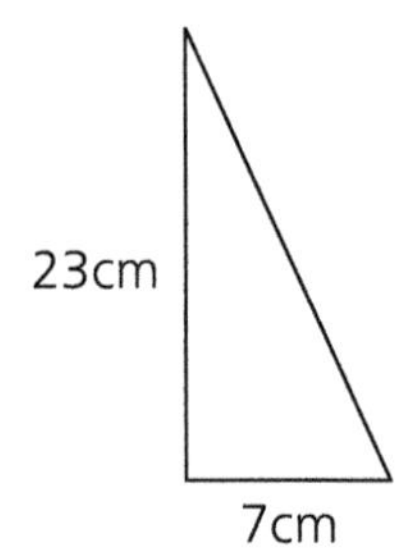

9 Find the area of this shape.

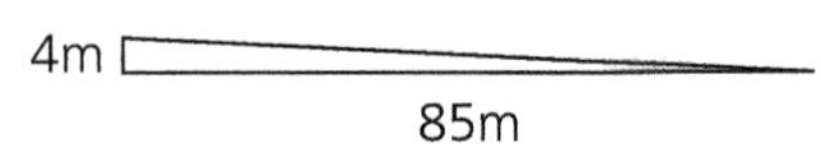

10 Find the area of this shape.

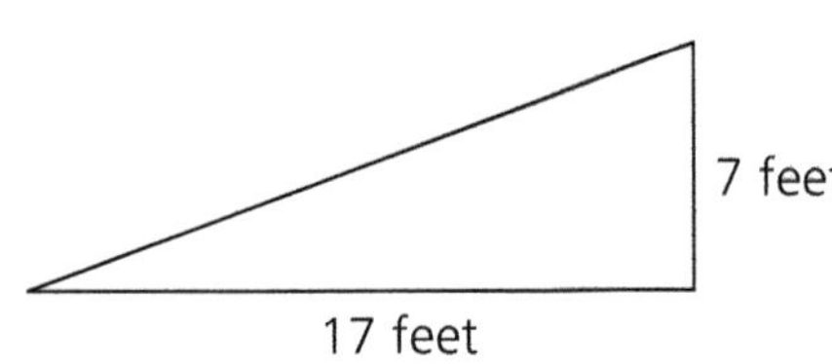

LESSON 11 PART 2: ANSWER SHEET

Mark your answer by putting a horizontal line in 1 of the boxes, as in the examples below.

Example 1:

10cm² ▭
40cm² ▭
14cm² ▭
20cm² ▬
6cm² ▭

Example 2:

64cm² ▭
128cm² ▬
96cm² ▭
192cm² ▭
32cm² ▭

1	2	3	4
30m ▭	59cm² ▭	28ft ▭	126m² ▭
40m ▭	75cm² ▭	29ft ▭	72m² ▭
50m ▭	120cm² ▭	48ft ▭	37m² ▭
60m ▭	24cm² ▭	49ft ▭	108m² ▭
70m ▭	31cm² ▭	52ft ▭	112m² ▭

5	6	7	8
44cm ▭	52m² ▭	26ft² ▭	30cm² ▭
162cm ▭	26m² ▭	16ft² ▭	161cm² ▭
54cm ▭	17m² ▭	105ft² ▭	80.5cm² ▭
52cm ▭	9m² ▭	52.5ft² ▭	70.5cm² ▭
36cm ▭	39m² ▭	50.5ft² ▭	16cm² ▭

9	10
89m² ▭	24ft² ▭
81m² ▭	10ft² ▭
340m² ▭	119ft² ▭
170m² ▭	55.5ft² ▭
21.5m² ▭	59.5ft² ▭

LESSON 12 Calculating Angles

In this exercise you'll be calculating angles. This shouldn't pose too many problems once you know the method. The key is to memorise certain facts and rules and then spot which one to use in the question.

Here are the key facts and rules you need to know:

1. There are 180° in a triangle.
2. A right angle is 90°.
3. An isosceles triangle has 2 equal sides and 2 equal angles.
4. An equilateral triangle has 3 equal sides and 3 equal angles.
5. There are 360° in a circle.
6. The angles in a quadrilateral add up to 360°.
7. An acute angle is smaller than 90°.
8. An obtuse angle is larger than 90° but smaller than 180°.
9. Angles on a straight line add up to 180°.
10. A reflex angle is larger than 180°.

There are quite a lot of rules there, but if you learn them, you'll quickly see how useful they are in a mathematics examination. Let's look at an example.

Example

What is angle B in the triangle below?

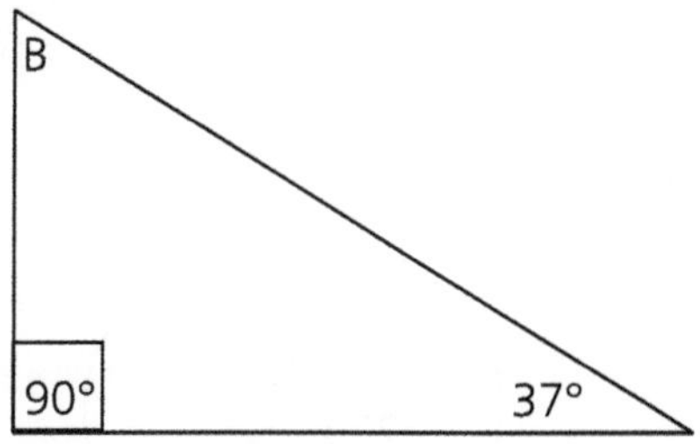

In this question, you must use your knowledge of triangles. You know that there are 180° in a triangle so to find the missing angle you simply need to do the following:

180° – 90° – 37° = 53°.

So your answer is 53°.

LESSON 12 PART 1

My Time

My Score

Now look at the questions below. Use your knowledge of angles to help you work out which numbers to use. Then mark your answers on the corresponding grids. You have 20 minutes to complete this task. Write the time you took and your score in the boxes above once you've finished.

1 A triangle has 3 angles, A, B and C. A is 78°, B is 43°, what is angle C?

2 A triangle has 3 angles: R which is a right angle, S which is 29° and T. What size is angle T?

3 This is an isosceles triangle and angles F and G are the same size. What size are they?

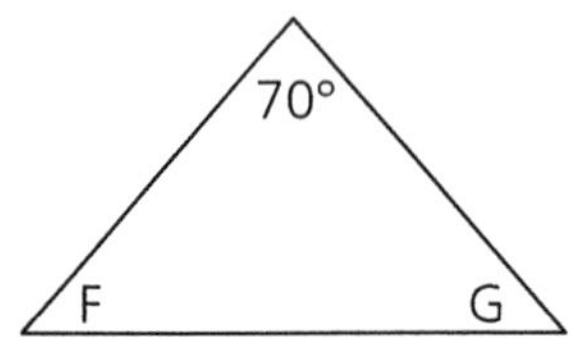

4 An equilateral triangle has 3 angles, X, Y and Z. How large is each angle?

5 Look at the shape below. What size is angle V?

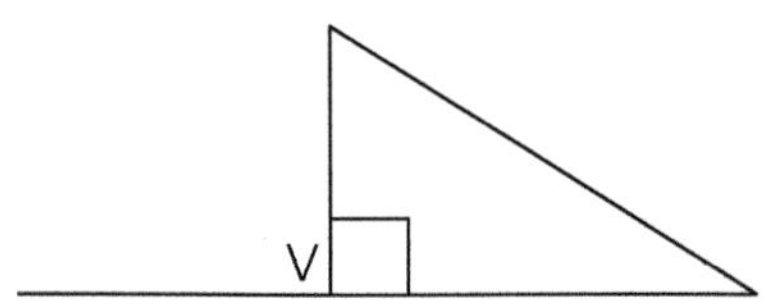

6 A round pizza is cut into 5 equal pieces. Each piece has the same angle at the centre of the pizza. What is this angle?

7 A triangle has 3 angles J, K and L. If J is 102°, K is 32°, what kind of angle is L?

8 Look at the triangle below. What kind of angle is X?

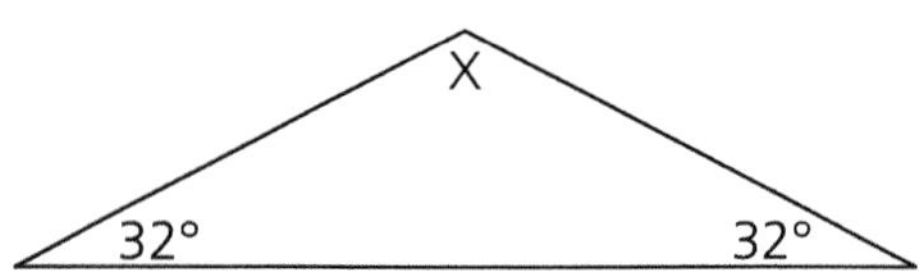

9 What size is angle P in the shape below?

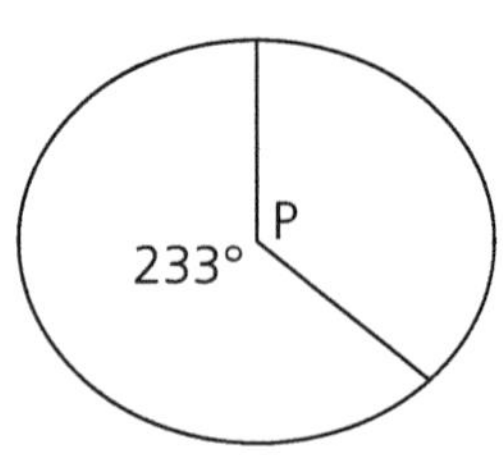

10 The minute hand of a clock starts at 12 and moves round to 3. Through how many degrees has it moved?

LESSON 12 PART 1: ANSWER SHEET

Mark your answer by putting a horizontal line in 1 of the boxes, as in the example below.

Example:

- 37° ☐
- 90° ☐
- 53° ☒
- 180° ☐
- 127° ☐

1
- 78° ☐
- 43° ☐
- 180° ☐
- 90° ☐
- 59° ☐

2
- 90° ☐
- 180° ☐
- 29° ☐
- 61° ☐
- 161° ☐

3
- 70° ☐
- 180° ☐
- 110° ☐
- 140° ☐
- 55° ☐

4
- 90° ☐
- 80° ☐
- 70° ☐
- 60° ☐
- 50° ☐

5
- 90° ☐
- 180° ☐
- 45° ☐
- 270° ☐
- 60° ☐

6
- 66° ☐
- 68° ☐
- 70° ☐
- 72° ☐
- 74° ☐

7
- Acute ☐
- Obtuse ☐
- Right ☐
- Straight ☐
- Reflex ☐

8
- Acute ☐
- Obtuse ☐
- Right ☐
- Straight ☐
- Reflex ☐

9
- 127° ☐
- 360° ☐
- 180° ☐
- 233° ☐
- 90° ☐

10
- 45° ☐
- 90° ☐
- 180° ☐
- 270° ☐
- 360° ☐

How Did You Do? Let's Find Out!

Here are the correct answers. You may mark your answers to these questions yourself.

1 59°

2 61°

3 55°

4 60°

5 90°

6 72°

7 Acute

8 Obtuse

9 127°

10 90°

If you scored 8 or more out of 10

This is great! This is a good score but if you scored 8 or 9, try to improve in the next part of the lesson. Check where you went wrong and make sure you learn your rules about angles. Look at the further hints on the next page before you move on to the next set of questions.

If you scored 6 to 7 out of 10

You need to improve on this score so keep practising – the hard work will pay off. Check which answers you got wrong. Also, check that you didn't make a mistake when marking your answers on the answer sheet. Read the further hints below and then move on to the next set of questions.

If you scored fewer than 6 out of 10

This is quite a low score so some more work is needed. Try to improve using the following advice before you move on to the next set of questions.

- ➪ Do you understand what to do? If not, get an adult to go over the instructions with you again. Then have a look at any questions you got wrong and try to understand why you didn't get the right answer. Make sure you do this thoroughly, as it will only get more difficult if you don't understand.

- ➪ Look at all of the rules about angles and make sure you learn and understand them all.

Further hints

- ➪ Sometimes you might see a shape with letters inside it instead of angles. Remember that if you see the same letter being used for two angles, those two angles will be exactly the same size.

- ➪ Remember that when you see a little box shape in one corner of a triangle, like the one I drew in question 5, it means it's a right angle and therefore its value is 90°.

LESSON 12 PART 2

My Time | **My Score**

Now let's try some more. Work through the questions and mark your answers on the corresponding grids. You have 20 minutes to complete this task. Remember to get an adult to mark these for you. Write the time you took and your score in the boxes above once you've finished.

1 A triangle has 3 angles, A, B and C. A is 58°, B is 63°, what is angle C?

2 If a quadrilateral has 3 angles of 42°, 59°, and 125°, what size is the fourth angle?

3 Look at the shape below. What size is angle K?

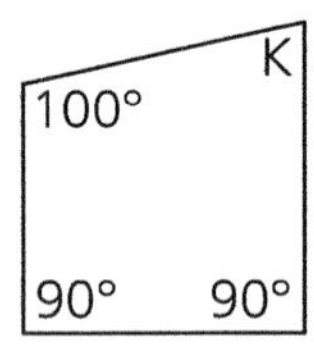

4 Shape ABCD is a square. How large is each angle?

5 Look at the shape below. What size is angle A?

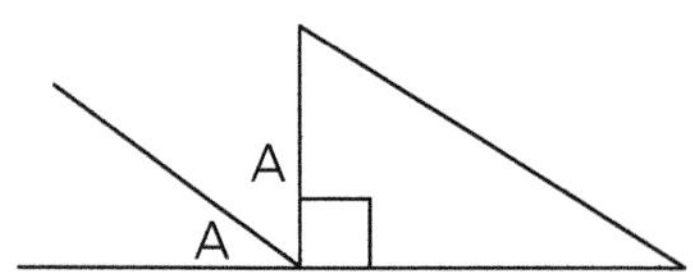

6 What is angle T worth?

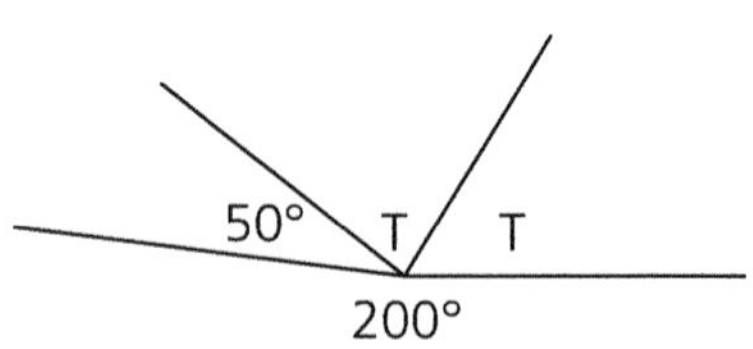

7 A triangle has angles of 28°, 28° and 124°. What kind of triangle is it?

8 Look at the triangle below. What kind of angle is angle Y?

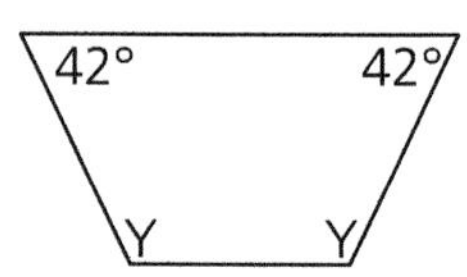

9 What size is angle Q in the shape below?

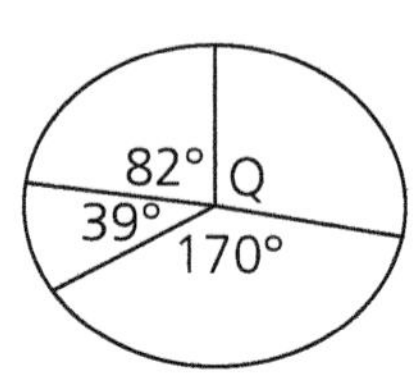

10 The minute hand of a clock starts at 1 and moves round to 5. Through how many degrees has it moved?

LESSON 12 PART 2: ANSWER SHEET

Mark your answer by putting a horizontal line in 1 of the boxes, as in the example below.

Example:

37° ▭
90° ▭
53° ▬
180° ▭
127° ▭

1
58° ▭
59° ▭
60° ▭
61° ▭
63° ▭

2
42° ▭
59° ▭
125° ▭
134° ▭
180° ▭

3
80° ▭
90° ▭
100° ▭
110° ▭
120° ▭

4
360° ▭
180° ▭
70° ▭
80° ▭
90° ▭

5
45° ▭
55° ▭
65° ▭
75° ▭
90° ▭

6
45° ▭
55° ▭
65° ▭
75° ▭
85° ▭

7
Acute ▭
Obtuse ▭
Equilateral ▭
Isosceles ▭
Right ▭

8
Acute ▭
Obtuse ▭
Straight ▭
Right ▭
Reflex ▭

9
39° ▭
82° ▭
170° ▭
69° ▭
99° ▭

10
45° ▭
90° ▭
100° ▭
120° ▭
180° ▭

LESSON 13 Multiplying Money and Decimals

In this exercise you'll need to be careful when multiplying, because the answers will often require a decimal point and you must get this in the right place. A good rule is to estimate the answer first so you've got an idea of what is reasonable, and then calculate your answer. This should make it easier to work out where the decimal point should go. Let's look at an example.

Example

What is 3.7 × 8.9?

For this question you can make a quick estimate to help you with the answer. (This is where knowledge of multiplication facts helps.) When you look at the question you should quickly round 3.7 up to 4 and 8.9 up to 9, then multiply to get a rough answer in your head. 4 × 9 = 36. You now know that your answer is going to be in the tens so you can use this to help you put your decimal point back in the right place at the end of your workings out.

To do this you then take the decimal points out and multiply the two numbers in the usual way.

$$\begin{array}{r} 8\,9 \\ \times\ 3\,7 \\ \hline 6\,2_{6}3 \\ +\ 2\,6_{2}7\,0 \\ \hline 3_{1}2\,9\,3 \end{array}$$

You now put your decimal point back in. You know from your estimate that your answer should be less than 36. So you can see that your actual answer should be <u>32.93</u>.

This is a really good way to check your answer is reasonable rather than simply doing calculations and assuming it is!

LESSON 13 PART 1

My Time

My Score

Now look at the questions below. Work them out on some scrap paper and then mark your answers on the corresponding grids. You have 20 minutes to complete this task. Write the time you took and your score in the boxes above once you've finished.

1 A plant grows 2.8mm each week. How much has it grown after 9 weeks?

2 A mobile phone contract costs £8.99 a month. How much does it cost for a year?

3 A car travels 13.6 miles in 15 minutes. How far will it travel in one hour?

4 Frasier spends 49p every day on a newspaper. How much does this cost him in a week?

5 Mr Winter prices out a school trip. It will cost each student £2.35. If 32 students go on the trip, how much money must he collect?

6 A bath holds 20 litres of water. If it fills up at the rate of half a litre every 10 minutes, how long will it take to get half full?

7 A garage contains 23 cars. If each car is 3.5m long, and the gap in between them is 0.2m, what length of space is needed for them all?

8 A shopkeeper spends £230 a week on new magazines. If each magazine sells for £4.20, how many must the shopkeeper sell to get his money back?

9 Shamila goes to dance school every Monday, Tuesday and Friday. Each lesson costs £3.25 and she attends for 12 weeks. How much money does she spend on her dance classes in total?

10 A runner drinks 1.3 litres of drink every 5 miles. How much drink does she consume after 20 miles?

LESSON 13 PART 1: ANSWER SHEET

Mark your answer by putting a horizontal line in 1 of the boxes, as in the example below.

Example:

11.16
5.2
32.93
24.63
27.56

1
3.7mm
18.9mm
25.2mm
18.72mm
22.5mm

2
£18.99
£24.99
£25.88
£107.88
£107.99

3
52.6 miles
195.6 miles
54.4 miles
204 miles
52.24 miles

4
£0.34
£3.43
£34.30
£34.03
£3.04

5
£64.35
£75.20
£2.67
£64.67
£34.35

6
20 minutes
20 hours
200 hours
2,000 minutes
3 hrs 20 mins

7
69.5m
69.7m
84.9m
80.5m
80.7m

8
53
54
55
56
57

9
£120.25
£119.00
£117.00
£117.25
£116.00

10
5.3 litres
26.3 litres
4.3 litres
6.5 litres
5.2 litres

How Did You Do? Let's Find Out!

Here are the correct answers. You may mark your answers to these questions yourself.

1 25.2mm

2 £107.88

3 54.4 miles

4 £3.43

5 £75.20

6 3 hrs 20 mins

7 84.9m

8 55

9 £117.00

10 5.2 litres

If you scored 8 or more out of 10

This is a good score but if you scored 8 or 9, try to improve in the next part of the lesson by checking where you went wrong and making sure you understand your mistakes. Look at the further hints on the next page before you move on to the next set of questions.

If you scored 6 to 7 out of 10

This score is okay, but to score higher next time try checking the answers you got wrong and also check that you didn't make a mistake when marking your answers on the sheet. Read the further hints below and then move on to the next set of questions.

If you scored fewer than 6 out of 10

Read the following advice to help you improve before you move on to the next set of questions.

➪ If you don't understand the instructions ask an adult to explain them to you. Then have a look at any questions you got wrong and try to understand why. Make sure you do this thoroughly, as it will only get more difficult if you don't understand.

➪ Read the further hints below before you move on.

Further hints

➪ Did you notice that in question 3 I gave a time proportion question with the decimal? Do remember that many questions will involve one or more mathematical processes. In question 3, you had to realise that to get your correct distance you would have to multiply by 4 since there are 4 lots of 15 minutes in an hour. So 4 × 13.6 = 54.4 miles.

➪ Did you notice that question 8 is one of those questions where you are given different pieces of information and you have to work out your answer in another way? In this question you have to work out how many groups of £4.20 will make £231. Dividing could be tricky since there is a decimal point involved so why not multiply £4.20 in groups?

First 10 groups of £4.20 = £42

Then multiply this by 5 to make 50 groups = £210

Now we're getting close. Another 5 groups of £4.20 = £21 your answer then is <u>55</u>.

➪ In question 7 there were 23 cars, but remember there would only be 22 gaps to measure since we'd need a car at either end. Watch out for questions like these!

LESSON 13 PART 2

My Time

My Score

Now let's try some more. Work the questions out on some scrap paper and then mark your answers on the opposite page. You have 20 minutes to complete this task. Write the time you took and your score in the boxes above once you've finished. Remember to get an adult to mark these for you.

1 A cyclist travels 37.3km every day for a week including the weekend. How far has she travelled by the end of the week?

2 If 13 people each measure exactly 1.72m, what is their combined height?

3 A shop sells 152 pairs of socks for 99p each. How much money does it make in total?

4 A plant grows 0.31mm every day during the month of May. How much has it grown by the end of this time?

5 A painter uses 1.23 litres of paint in each room of a large house. If he paints 23 rooms, how much paint does he use in total?

6 A day out at Superland fun park costs £12.50 for an adult and £6.30 for a child. If Mr Salisbury took his wife and 3 children, how much did it cost him to go to the fun park in total?

7 Denzel has £30 to spend from his birthday money. How many computer games can he buy if 1 computer game costs £7.49?

8 Fastville motor racing track measures 1.67 miles. If a car completes 42 laps in a race, how far does it travel in all?

9 Mr Melville wants to grow his own garlic. He must plant the seeds 25mm apart from each other and from the sides of the pot. If his pot is 110cm long, how many seeds can he plant in his pot?

10 A charity walk is 3.4km long. If 86 people take part, what will be the total combined distance covered by all the walkers?

LESSON 13 PART 2: ANSWER SHEET

Mark your answer by putting a horizontal line in 1 of the boxes, as in the example below.

Example:

11.16
5.2
32.93
24.63
27.56

1
44.3km
261.1km
259.3km
38km
260km

2
1.85m
13.72m
14.72m
22.36m
22.72m

3
£150.48
£152.99
£15.48
£1504.80
£1.50

4
9.61mm
31.31mm
9.3mm
30.31mm
0.62mm

5
23.23 litres
23.46 litres
28.29 litres
28.23 litres
24.23 litres

6
£18.80
£31.30
£31.40
£43.90
£37.80

7
2
3
4
5
6

8
42.67 miles
43.67 miles
70.67 miles
70.14 miles
2.09 miles

9
40
41
42
43
44

10
89.4km
267.4km
3.90km
292.4km
91.46km

LESSON 14 Finding Averages and Ranges

In this exercise you'll need to understand the difference between all 3 types of average or a range and how to calculate each one. Let's have a look at each type and then you can try some examples.

Mean

This type of average requires you to add up all the numbers that you have been given and then divide your answer by the amount of numbers. If a question simply states 'Find the average', you should calculate the mean.

Median

This type of average requires you firstly to place all the numbers you have in order of size from smallest to biggest. Where a number occurs more than once, you must write it more than once. Then you simply count along and find the number that appears in the middle of the list. If there is no one number in the middle you must take the two numbers which are closest and find the mean of these (add them together and divide them by 2).

Mode

This type of average is similar to the median in that you should first place all of the numbers in order of size from smallest to biggest. Then you simply check which number occurs most often, and that number is the mode.

Range

The range is not an average. It simply tells you the difference between the largest and smallest numbers you have. So you simply subtract the smallest number from the largest.

Example

For the following set of numbers you need to find all 3 averages and the range. (A question in an examination would only ask you to find 1 or 2 at most.)

2, 7, 4, 9, 8, 6, 5, 1, 4, 4, 5

The mean: add up all the numbers = 55
there are 11 numbers, so divide by 11. 55 ÷ 11 = 5

The mean = 5

The median: put all the numbers in order: 1, 2, 4, 4, 4, 5, 5, 6, 7, 8, 9
there are 11 numbers so the middle number is the 6th one.

The 6th number is 5

The median = 5

The mode: put the numbers in order: 1, 2, 4, 4, 4, 5, 5, 6, 7, 8, 9
the one that occurs most often is 4

The mode = 4

The range: subtract the smallest number from the largest: 9 – 1 = 8

The range = 8

LESSON 14 PART 1

My Time

My Score

Now look at the questions below. Work them out on some scrap paper and then mark your answers on the corresponding grids. You have 20 minutes to complete this task. Write the time you took and your score in the boxes above once you've finished.

1. Three children are given pocket money of £5, £4 and £6. What is the median average pocket money?

2. What is the median height of 5 plants measuring 6.3cm, 5.7cm, 8.2cm, 6.9cm and 7.1cm in height.

3. Rotchester Rovers played 8 matches in 1 season. They scored the following number of goals in each match: 2, 0, 1, 0, 3, 1, 1, 4. What is the mode of the number of goals they scored in 1 season?

4. The children at Happy Primary School scored 10, 12, 7, 15, 18, 3 out of 20 in a spelling test. What is the range of their scores?

5. In a busy market, traders are selling bags of beans. What is the median number of beans per bag, if the bags contain 212, 321, 405, 326, 341 beans each?

6. The weight of 8 suitcases, recorded at an airport is 12kg, 14kg, 11kg, 23kg, 12kg, 19kg, 12kg, 20kg. What is the mode?

7. What is the mean of the following number of pages in books: 234, 128, 208, 322, 458?

8. Find the range of the following amounts of money: £2.17, £5.19, £6.03, £3.12, £4.08.

9. A, B, C, D and E are 5 children who collect stickers. A collects 20, B 23, C 18 and D 9. The mean of their stickers is 17 so how many stickers does E have?

10. The fish tanks in a pet shop contain the following number of fish: 7, 18, 9, 4, 7, 8, 12, 15, 6. What is the median?

LESSON 14 PART 1: ANSWER SHEET

Mark your answer by putting a horizontal line in 1 of the boxes for each question.

1	2	3	4
£3	6.3cm	0	17
£4	5.7cm	1	16
£5	8.2cm	2	15
£6	6.9cm	3	14
£7	7.1cm	4	13

5	6	7	8
405	12kg	230	£2.17
341	11kg	240	£3.12
321	20kg	250	£4.14
326	23kg	260	£4.04
212	14kg	270	£3.86

9	10
14	12
15	15
16	7
17	8
18	9

How Did You Do? Let's Find Out!

Here are the correct answers. You may mark your answers to these questions yourself.

1. £5
2. 6.9cm
3. 1
4. 15
5. 326
6. 12kg
7. 270
8. £3.86
9. 15
10. 8

If you scored 8 or more out of 10

If you scored 8 or 9, try to improve in the next part of the lesson by checking where you went wrong here and looking at the further hint on the next page before you move on to the next set of questions.

If you scored 6 to 7 out of 10

This score is okay, but try to score higher next time. Check the answers you got wrong. Also, check that you didn't make a mistake when marking your answers on the grid. Read the further hint below and then move on to the next set of questions.

If you scored fewer than 6 out of 10

With a bit more hard work I'm sure you can improve your score. Before you move on to the next set of questions, read the following advice to help you improve.

- Do you understand what to do? If not, get an adult to go over the instructions with you again. Then have a look at any questions you got wrong and try to understand why. Make sure you do this thoroughly, as it will only get more difficult if you don't understand.

- Do you understand how to calculate each type of average and also the range? Make sure you learn them all thoroughly before you proceed.

- Read the further hint below before you move on.

Further hint

- Once again I put in a question requiring you to use inverse operations. Remember inverse operations mean we have to do things the other way around. Look again at question 9. In this question I told you what the average was and 4 of the 5 scores. In order to calculate the final score, first you must find the total, which would be the average multiplied by the number of children:

  $5 \times 17 = 85$

  Next, add up the numbers you have:

  So $20 + 23 + 18 + 9 = 70$

  Now, take this away from the total.

  $85 - 70 = \underline{15}$, which is your answer.

  Watch out for these.

LESSON 14 PART 2

My Time

My Score

Now let's try some more. Work the questions out on some scrap paper and then mark your answers on the corresponding grids. You have 20 minutes to complete this task. Remember to get an adult to mark these for you. Write the time you took and your score in the boxes above once you've finished.

1 A car drives the following number of miles each day for a week: 12, 35, 23, 67, 88, 14 and 37. What is the median distance it has travelled in a week?

2 A total of 5 children took part in the long jump at school. Their jumps measured: 3.4m, 2.5m, 3.7m, 3.6m and 1.8m. What is the mean?

3 If the range of a car's top speed is 78mph and the slowest recorded speed was 14mph, what was its fastest speed?

4 Three houses are sold for: £120,000, £95,000 and £85,000. What is the mean price?

5 The height of 5 mountains is 1,035m, 22,306m, 43,015m, 5,607m, 2,078m. What is the median height?

6 The total weight of 5 people in a lift is 600kg. What is their average weight?

7 The number of tickets sold for a play each night of the week is as follows: Monday 23, Tuesday 45, Wednesday 36, Thursday 45, Friday 62, Saturday 67, Sunday 20. What is the mode?

8 The average length of 6 pieces of string is 7cm. If the first 5 measure 3cm, 1cm, 4cm, 9cm and 12cm, what does the sixth measure?

9 Ashley measured the temperature in his room for 5 days at: 12°C, 17°C, 23°C, 18°C, and 21°C. What is the median temperature over the 5 days?

10 Find the range of these numbers: 3.72, 8.06, 1.49, 5.03, 6.7, 1.3.

LESSON 14 PART 2: ANSWER SHEET

Mark your answer by putting a horizontal line in 1 of the boxes for each question.

1
- 14
- 37
- 23
- 35
- 12

2
- 3.0m
- 3.1m
- 3.2m
- 3.3m
- 3.4m

3
- 92mph
- 64mph
- 14mph
- 78mph
- 62mph

4
- £120,000
- £110,000
- £100,000
- £90,000
- £80,000

5
- 22,306m
- 1,035m
- 2,078m
- 43,015m
- 5,607m

6
- 100kg
- 110kg
- 120kg
- 130kg
- 140kg

7
- 45
- 23
- 67
- 62
- 20

8
- 10cm
- 11cm
- 12cm
- 13cm
- 14cm

9
- 12°C
- 23°C
- 18°C
- 17°C
- 21°C

10
- 6.76
- 5.4
- 6.4
- 5.76
- 6.67

LESSON 15 Finding a Percentage of a Number

For these questions you have to calculate the percentage of a whole number. I'll show you a quick method which will help you work these out if the percentage you need to find is a factor of 100.

Let's first remind ourselves of the factors of 100.

They are: 1, 2, 4, 5, 10, 20, 25, 50, 100,

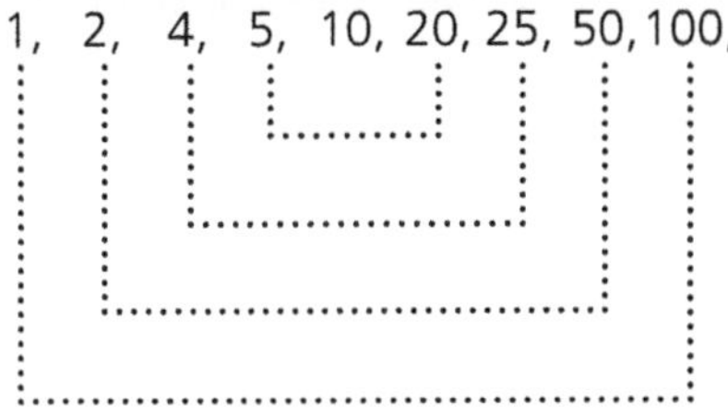

The factors of 100 all pair up to make 100 and you can use this to your advantage.

So, 1 × 100, 2 × 50, 4 × 25, 5 × 20 and then 10 pairs with itself, 10 × 10.

If you are asked to find 25% of a number, look at the number which you multiply 25 by to make 100. As you can see it's 4.

You now divide your number by 4 and you have found 25%. Let's look at an example:

Example

Find 25% of 88.

Divide 88 by 4. This is 22, so <u>22</u> is 25% of 88. This is the answer you mark on your answer grid.

HELPFUL HINT

Make sure you learn all of those factors of 100 off by heart – they'll save you loads of time in an exam!

LESSON 15 PART 1

My Time

My Score

Let's try some more questions. Work out the answers on some scrap paper and then mark them on the answer sheet. You have 20 minutes to complete this task. Write the time you took and your score in the boxes above once you've finished.

1. If a factory makes 780 cars and 10% are yellow, how many cars are yellow?
2. Of a class of 32 children, 50% walked to school. How many is this?
3. Of 130 people in a restaurant, 20% order soup. How many do not order soup?
4. A savings account earns 2% on £300. How much money is this?
5. A shopping bill comes to £87.00 but 10% is taken off. What is the new bill?
6. Brandi scored 75% on her spelling test. If the test was out of 20, what was her actual score?
7. A greengrocer sells fruit and vegetables. If he sells 200 items and 4% of these are potatoes, how many potatoes does he sell in total?
8. A football team has a squad of 24 players. If 25% are injured, how many players are uninjured?
9. On Sunday, 20% of shoppers in a supermarket carried baskets. If this was 48 shoppers, how many people were shopping in the supermarket that day?
10. If 80 people went to a doctor's surgery and 5% had a cold, how many people was this?

LESSON 15 PART 1: ANSWER SHEET

Mark your answer by putting a horizontal line in 1 of the boxes, as in the example below.

Example:

18 ▭
20 ▭
22 ▬
24 ▭
28 ▭

1	2	3	4
780	3.2	13	£2
78	15	26	£4
7.8	16	39	£6
0.78	27	52	£8
87	17	104	£10

5	6	7	8
£8.70	5	4	6
£87.00	10	8	12
£79.30	12	12	15
£78.30	15	16	18
£77.30	17	20	20

9	10
4.8	8
9.6	7
240	6
68	5
480	4

How Did You Do? Let's Find Out!

Here are the correct answers. You may mark your answers to these questions yourself.

1 78

2 16

3 104

4 £6

5 £78.30

6 15

7 8

8 18

9 240

10 4

If you scored 8 or more out of 10

This is a good score – well done! If you scored 8 or 9, try to improve in the next part of the lesson by checking where you went wrong and by looking at the further hints on the next page before you move on to the next set of questions.

If you scored 6 to 7 out of 10

This score is okay, but you'll need to score higher next time. Check which answers you got wrong and see if you can work out why this happened. Also, check that you didn't make a mistake when marking your answers on the sheet. Read the further hints below and then move on to the next set of questions.

If you scored fewer than 6 out of 10

Make sure you understand factors and how to find them. Look at lesson 4 if you're unsure about factors. Read the further hints below before you move on.

Further hints

➪ What happens if you need to find 70% of an amount? As 70 is not a factor of 100, this means you have to use a 2 step method. In this case, you find 10% and then multiply this by 7 to find 70%. Let's look at some examples to see how it works.

Example 1

Find 70% of £3.40

First divide £3.40 by 10 to find 10% so £3.40 ÷ 10 = £0.34

Then multiply the answer by 7 to find 70% so £0.34 x 7 = <u>£2.38</u>

Example 2

Find 11% of £86.00

Find 10% so £86.00 ÷ 10 = £8.60

Now divide this answer by 10 again to find 1% so £8.60 ÷ 10 = £0.86

Finally, add the2 answers together, so £8.60 + £0.86 = <u>£9.46</u>

➪ If you can, find 10% first as it's easy and then work from there.

LESSON 15 PART 2

My Time

My Score

Now let's try some more. Work the questions out on some scrap paper and then mark your answers on the corresponding grids. You have 20 minutes to complete this task. Remember to get an adult to mark these for you. Write the time you took and your score in the boxes above once you've finished.

1. A school took 20% of its children to the theatre. If there are 460 children in the school, how many went to the theatre?
2. Of 300 people working at a factory, 4% are ill one day. How many people is this?
3. Olive's shopping bill is £38.40. She is given a 5% discount for being a loyal customer. How much is her new bill?
4. An aeroplane can carry 270 passengers. If 20% of the seats are empty for one flight, how many passengers are on board?
5. A restaurant has 140 meals on its menu, of which 25% are vegetarian. How many meals are vegetarian?
6. Bela, a teacher, calculates that 15% of his 220 pens have run dry. How many pens is this?
7. A football manager works out that Roody, his top striker, scored 40% of his team's goals last season. If the team scored 60 goals, how many did Roody score?
8. A mobile phone shop offers a 22% discount on phones that cost £70. How much money does this save the customer?
9. If a car fuel gauge shows that it is 20% full when it has 7 litres of petrol in its tank, how many litres can the car hold when its tank is completely full?
10. Of 150 people in a café, 8% want ketchup on their chips. How many people did not choose this option?

LESSON 15 PART 2: ANSWER SHEET

Mark your answer by putting a horizontal line in 1 of the boxes, as in the example below.

Example:

- 18
- 20
- 22 (marked)
- 24
- 28

1
- 440
- 46
- 66
- 92
- 100

2
- 4
- 8
- 12
- 16
- 20

3
- £3.84
- £1.92
- £34.56
- £36.48
- £38.68

4
- 27
- 54
- 250
- 243
- 216

5
- 115
- 35
- 70
- 105
- 25

6
- 11
- 22
- 33
- 44
- 55

7
- 20
- 22
- 24
- 26
- 28

8
- £48.00
- £16.00
- £15.40
- £14.00
- £3.40

9
- 13 litres
- 27 litres
- 140 litres
- 14 litres
- 35 litres

10
- 8
- 142
- 12
- 138
- 15

SCORE SHEET

To find a percentage of a mark out of 10, simply multiply your score by 10 – but you should know this already by now!

LESSON	Part 1 score	Part 1 percent	Part 2 score	Part 2 percent
1				
2				
3				
4				
5				
6				
7				
8				
9				
10				
11				
12				
13				
14				
15				
Average				

Metric measures

10 millimetres (mm) = 1 centimetre (cm)
100 centimetres (cm) = 1 metre (m)
1,000 millimetres (mm) = 1 metre (m)

1,000 metres (m) = 1 kilometre (km)
1,000 millilitres (ml) = 1 litre (l)
1,000 grams (g) = 1 kilogram (kg)

To convert:
mm to cm divide by 10
cm to mm multiply by 10
mm to m divide by 1,000
m to mm multiply by 1,000
cm to m divide by 100
m to cm multiply by 100

m to km divide by 1,000
km to m multiply by 1,000
g to kg divide by 1,000
kg to g multiply by 1,000
ml to l divide by 1,000
l to ml multiply by 1,000

VOCABULARY BUILDER

Use this page to write down any new words you've learnt in this book. Look up the meaning of each in a dictionary, so that you'll know what they mean in future.

New word	Meaning

AND FINALLY...

Firstly, let me begin by saying 'well done'. You must have worked hard to complete this book, especially on top of your other homework from school!

Now that you've completed the first maths book in the Practise & Pass 11+ series, it's time to take stock. Have a look back at your scores and make a note of the kinds of questions you found quite straightforward and scored well on, and those that you found more difficult and didn't score so well on. Taking a maths paper is all about strategy so if you know you can complete some questions quickly and get them right, then you know that this will give you more time for those you find a bit trickier.

Make sure you read back over the methods for each question – these will serve you well during your examination. When you're ready, move on to the next book (*Practise & Pass 11+ Level Two: Develop Maths*) which features more types of maths questions. In that book I also show you how to speed up, with tips and tricks on how to use those multiple choice grids.

And don't forget, if you need help with non-verbal reasoning, verbal reasoning or English, there are books for each of those to help you prepare for your exams:

- ⇨ *Practise & Pass 11+ Level One: Discover English*
- ⇨ *Practise & Pass 11+ Level One: Discover Verbal Reasoning*
- ⇨ *Practise & Pass 11+ Level One: Discover Non-Verbal Reasoning*
- ⇨ *Practise & Pass 11+ Level Two: Develop English*
- ⇨ *Practise & Pass 11+ Level Two: Develop Verbal Reasoning*
- ⇨ *Practise & Pass 11+ Level Two: Develop Non-Verbal Reasoning*
- ⇨ *Practise & Pass 11+ Level Three: Practice Test Papers*

Keep working and good luck!

ANSWERS TO PART 2 QUESTIONS

LESSON 1

1. 40,000
2. 9 hundredths
3. 300
4. 8 hundredths
5. 3 tenths
6. 500,000
7. 4 thousandths
8. 100,000
9. 3 tenths
10. 6 hundredths

LESSON 2

1. 40
2. 210
3. 48
4. 21
5. 620
6. 229
7. 35
8. 48
9. 1 fifth
10. 1 sixth

LESSON 3

1. 18
2. 65
3. 30
4. 55
5. 55 litres
6. 420
7. 85
8. 12,800ml
9. 210 pages
10. 44

LESSON 4

1. $^{18}/_{31}$
2. $^{5}/_{16}$
3. $^{3}/_{10}$
4. $^{2}/_{5}$
5. $^{1}/_{4}$
6. $^{3}/_{13}$
7. $^{3}/_{8}$
8. $^{1}/_{3}$
9. $^{4}/_{5}$
10. $^{1}/_{2}$

LESSON 5

1. £94.50
2. 28.13 miles
3. 1.19 seconds
4. 4.72m
5. £3.43
6. 0.191km
7. 961g
8. 1.39m
9. 1.047 litres
10. £9.91

LESSON 6

1. 50%
2. 40%
3. 7
4. 80%
5. 20%
6. 75%
7. 50%
8. 40
9. 75%
10. 20%

LESSON 7

1. $^{1}/_{5}$
2. $^{3}/_{40}$
3. $^{1}/_{10}$
4. $^{1}/_{8}$
5. $^{7}/_{40}$
6. $^{13}/_{40}$
7. $^{5}/_{8}$
8. $^{1}/_{4}$

9. $^1/_2$
10. $^1/_4$

LESSON 8

1. 200
2. 20
3. 17:16
4. £15
5. 50
6. 20:17
7. 24:19
8. 14
9. 7
10. 14

LESSON 9

1. £0.84
2. 45 tonnes
3. 95km
4. 46p
5. 70p
6. £0.56
7. £100
8. 39
9. 180g
10. £1.10

LESSON 10

1. 24m
2. 5
3. 45cm
4. $14m^2$
5. 5cm
6. $361m^2$
7. 7m
8. 30m, 7m
9. 14m, 20m
10. $62m^2$

LESSON 11

1. 40m
2. $59cm^2$
3. 52ft
4. $108m^2$
5. 54cm
6. $26m^2$
7. $52.5ft^2$
8. $80.5cm^2$
9. $170m^2$
10. $59.5ft^2$

LESSON 12

1. 59°
2. 134°
3. 80°
4. 90°
5. 45°
6. 55°
7. isosceles
8. obtuse
9. 69°
10. 120°

LESSON 13

1. 261.1km
2. 22.36m
3. £150.48
4. 9.61mm
5. 28.29 litres
6. £43.90
7. 4
8. 70.14 miles
9. 43
10. 292.4km

LESSON 14

1. 35
2. 3.0m
3. 92mph
4. £100,000
5. 5,607m
6. 120kg
7. 45
8. 13cm
9. 18°C
10. 6.76

LESSON 15

1. 92
2. 12
3. £36.48
4. 216
5. 35
6. 33
7. 24
8. £15.40
9. 35 litres
10. 138